**PRAISE ~~FOR CRUCIFIED~~**

"*Crucified to Life* is a challenging, yet encouraging read. My friend Brandon Kelley pulls no punches when it comes to sharing biblical truth; yet his upbeat and positive personality shines through in his writing style. Chock-full of examples and characters from the Bible, as well as relatable personal illustrations, the book reads as if you are having a conversation with a friend over coffee. As the subtitle describes, it paints a picture of what it looks like to have abundant life in Christ. I recommend it for seekers, new believers, as well as long-time Christ-followers who need a reminder of the goodness of the Lord."

- Mike Kjergaard, Lead Minister of Christ's Hope Ministries and Church

"Brandon Kelley has a heart for discipleship that excites me. He is a passionate husband, dad, pastor, friend, and writer and this comes out on every page of *Crucified to Life*. Brandon wants us all to understand grace and has been given a special ability to not only identify common pitfalls but to point a way out. This book is a great read for Christians who want to be both challenged and encouraged as they accept their identity in Christ and their call to different living. Personally, I am fortunate to call Brandon a friend and thankful that his book allows others to glimpse into the life of a pastor who loves people and wants the best for them. If you want to experience the fullness of a life in Christ, this book is for you."

- Nathan Hardesty, Senior Minister of Bridgetown Church of Christ

"Brandon Kelley understands the backwards, upside down, subversive nature of the abundant life. Everyone wants the full life that Christ came to give, but what does that look like? How do we know that we have it? This book opens up the topic, explores the heart of the issue, and with surgeon-like precision, cuts away at the assumptions in our way. In the end, having left in view what it really looks like to have the abundant life."

- Clarence Garrett (aka T.A.G.), Hip-Hop Recording Artist and Co-Founder of Light Rider Music

"Brandon Kelley has combined good theology and practical application in writing his new book, *Crucified to Life*. The book speaks to several topics that need to be on the preaching and teaching list of church leaders everywhere. This book can also be a great resource for small group studies. I definitely recommend the purchase of this work for your ministry and personal walk with Christ."

- Dr. David Roadcup, Professor of Discipleship of TCMI International

"In a culture that craves simple answers and easy fixes, Brandon Kelley gives us the exact opposite in *Crucified to Life*. He leads us to embrace this paradox of following Jesus: the only way to really live is to die. Brandon connects the ancient text of Scripture with life in the 21st century, inviting us to step into the paradoxical, but wonderful, way of Jesus. It's the way of the crucified. It's the way to life.

- Mike Edmisten, Senior Pastor of Connect Christian Church

# CRUCIFIED TO LIFE

*What Abundant Life in Christ Really Looks Like*

Brandon Kelley

**Crucified to Life:**

What Abundant Life in Christ Really Looks Like

Copyright © 2017 by Brandon Kelley

ISBN-13: 978-1542790888
ISBN-10: 1542790883

Printed in the United States of America

## FREE BONUS RESOURCES

For all readers: If you would like to dive deeper into this journey of the abundant life, grab your copy of the *Crucified to Life 30-Day Bible Reading Plan.* You can get it by going to BrandonKelley.org/bonus.

For pastors: If you would like to share *Crucified to Life* with your congregation, you'll want to get your copy of the *Crucified to Life Sermon Series Pack.* In it are four message outlines and all the graphics you need to help your congregation live abundant life in Christ. You can get it by going to BrandonKelley.org/pastors.

*For my grandparents, parents, siblings, wife, and children. I love you all. May this book deepen your relationship with Christ.*

# Table of Contents

# FOREWORD

It was Super Bowl Sunday, February 2011. I was leaving church and was walking out to my car when I received a phone call, it was from Brandon Kelley. He stated that something had happened during service that day and he and Sara wanted to get together and talk, it was important. I asked if it was not an emergency, could it wait until the beginning of the week? Brandon said yes, and we met early in the week.

When I met with Brandon and Sara they stated that the Lord had challenged them to do something with ministry last Sunday and they were looking for my input and guidance on what to do next. I suggested that they check out Cincinnati Christian University sometime and see what they thought. Little did I know that they scheduled a campus visit for the next weekend. Long story short. They said yes to Cincinnati, they quit their jobs, and moved down to CCU in a very short time. As I like to say, they "climbed on the God Rocket, lit it and never looked back!"

There is so much I could say about Brandon and Sara, but let me try and boil it down to this. When they commit to something they are "all in." Whether it was involvement with our church family and their Sunday School class, the jobs they had, the sales organization they were involved in, or their love and commitment to each other, they were, and are both, "all in."

Over the past 8 years or so, I have been able to witness this passion for God and His truth grow. As I read *Crucified to Life* I could see the lives of Brandon and Sara jumping off the pages, I could hear his voice as I read this book.

Being crucified to Christ means living a crucified life, it means living a life completely sold out and formed into the image of the Savior. As I read this book I was drawn deeper into what a great gift we have been given. The gift of eternal life! Jesus, through the mercy and grace of the Father, has paid our debt and we can stand in front of the Father clean and whole.

As we journey through Jesus' words on the sermon on the mountainside (Matthew 5-7) we take a "deeper dive," we don't just hit the "popular" or "common" texts, but we are led into the deep end of the pool, not in an academic way, but in a deep, personal, passionate way. Brandon reminds us that the cost of following Jesus is a life crucified to ourselves, it is a life that leans into "hard things," it is a life worth living. Through personal examples, stories, and good scholarship, we get a picture of what following Jesus really looks like.

This book challenged me to "get off the nickel" to stop "playing it safe" and lean into the real life I was called to in Christ. This book does not just tell us what we should do, it reminds us of whose we are, and what abundant life in Christ really looks like!

Brandon, thank you for letting the Lord use you in this way and Sara thank you for loving Brandon and co-authoring this journey with him.

- Greg Krafft, Lead Minister of Cedar Creek Church

# Author's Note

An aha moment. You know when you have one. It's that moment when something *clicks* in your mind. It's that moment when what used to be confusing, now makes sense. My hope and my prayer is that this book will open the door to an "aha moment" for you.

You may ask, what is this book about? To that, let me start with what it's not about. This book is not about a *deeper Christianity*. This book is not about a feel-good faith that always turns out *happily ever after* (at least not in this world). Instead, this book is about the Christianity we should all know and live, but sadly, we may have missed altogether.

We have misunderstood grace; we have misunderstood the good news. We have let the Gospel stop at God saving us from Hell. And, yet, it is much more than that. The work that God has done and is doing is more than that, and it is my hope and prayer that through this book, more people (including you) will discover what abundant life in Christ really looks like.

New Christians and those who are unsure about Christianity will find this book to be a resource that will help them build a foundation of what the Christian life is all about. If you are unsure about Christianity, I highly recommend that you ask a Christian friend or a local pastor to read this book with you and to discuss the content together.

Christians who struggle to read the Bible consistently will find this book to be a doorway to the joy of knowing what God has done and is doing in their lives.

Christians who are well read and who read the Bible consistently will find this book to become *deeper* as each chapter builds on each other.

The majority of this book is written with the assumption that you have already committed your life to Christ and now are asking, "what's next?"

## Organization

I have organized this book in two very important sections. Section one is "The Reality of the Crucified." In this section, we will explore the Gospel in its fullness. We won't stop at God saving us from eternal damnation.

Instead, we'll see the Gospel in all its beauty and, by doing so, we'll discover a foundation for the next section.

Section two is "The Way of the Crucified." We'll see how our activity follows our reality. We'll dive deep into what a Christ follower looks like on an everyday level. By the end of section two, we'll have a clear picture of what living in Christ looks like on an everyday level.

Both sections combined are necessary for us to realize what abundant life in Christ really looks like. He came to give us life that is far beyond what we could ever imagine.

## Christian Living or Theology?

There seems to be a belief in modern Christian literature that the genres of *Christian Living* and *Theology* don't belong together. I disagree. We can't have a proper understanding of the Christian life without a proper understanding of theology.

If I've succeeded in this endeavor, you'll find the blending of both genres and you'll see that both are meant to be in the same conversation.

As you flip these pages and begin this journey, know that I am praying for you. And even though I may not know you, the One to whom I am praying does know you. He knows you more than you could ever comprehend. And to make that even better, He not only knows you but He also loves you.

# SECTION ONE: THE REALITY OF THE CRUCIFIED

CHAPTER 1

# CHRISTIAN MUSLIMS AND THE CRUCIFIED GOD

*We are saved, not by some fine theory and not by some blinding revelation and certainly not by our own best effort, but by Christ's atoning death. – Leon Morris*

Well-known pastor and author, Andy Stanley, asked this question in a sermon: "What do you think about when you think about what God thinks about you?" This question is a powerful one because how we answer it says a lot about how we view God. What we believe about God determines how we live for God. So, what comes to mind for you?

## CONSTANT QUESTIONS

Thinking back to my childhood, I have little recollection of talking about God with my family. I can remember going to a Lutheran church with my dad every other weekend, but only for a short time. My experience there can be summed up into one word: boredom.

As I moved into my high school years, I fell into a bedtime ritual that took place almost every night. I would lay down, turn on a movie, and after the movie was over, lay silently with my mind wandering. Twisting. Turning. Contemplating. My mind raced constantly at one thing: what in the world am I here for? That question was just the beginning of my search for meaning and purpose. It led to more questions like, if I am just going to be on this earth, living this life for a hundred years or so, then what's the point? and, what is the purpose in just existing and dying? which then led to, why am I here if there was no point in the first place? A purposeless existence didn't make much sense to me. After racing through these questions on a nightly basis, I would pray. I didn't know to whom I was praying exactly, but somehow I knew I was praying to God.

This internal battle continued into college. I remember talking with my grandparents about why we exist and my grandmother bought me a book called, *Heaven and the Afterlife*. I never did read that book, but it sits on my bookshelf just a couple feet away from me. I was searching for answers. Have you been there? Have you ever questioned your existence? I think it's a healthy thing to question. It was for me, anyway. The real question we're asking when we question our existence, though, is this: Does God exist, and if He does, what is He really like?

## A RIDICULOUS ANSWER

Yes. God exists. You were not brought into this world by chance. You were not a mistake no matter what people may have told you. You have value because God has given you value. He has given you a purpose. He cares deeply for you. When you rebel against Him, He is yearning to embrace you. When you are hurting, He is mourning with you. The God I want to tell you about is the crucified God, for He is the one true God.

Imagine this: The Creator of the Universe loves you. Yes, you. Don't you dare gloss over that reality. The world says you were an accident; God says you are loved. Which do you believe?

I follow the God who loves us so much that He decided to come down to earth, become a man, and willingly sacrifice Himself for the sake of our forgiveness. That is ridiculous, I know. It's ridiculous that God would do such a thing, that He would leave Heavenly glory and embrace humanity for the sake of redeeming you and me. It's crazy. It's crazy *awesome* because it's true.

Your sin and my sin created a problem. The Holy God who demands a standard of perfection is confronted with sin. He must punish that sin. The problem is, in addition to being holy, He is also love, not just loving, but *love*. It is part of God's nature. These two attributes within God must be reconciled. He must punish our sin, yet He must also express love. What does He do? He offers Himself to become a curse for us. He takes the debt that we owe to Him and pays it on our behalf. Our debt is wiped clean through the blood of Jesus.

## CRUCIFIED TO DEATH

The death of Jesus was the mission of Jesus. He came to earth with the sole purpose of saving those who are lost. It was God's plan of redemption that Jesus willingly offered Himself in our place on the cross.

His death was payment for our sin – past, present, and future. We need not wonder whether we are forgiven or not if we are in Christ Jesus. We need not think that we can gain salvation by our own works, "for all have sinned and fall short of the glory of God, and are justified by his grace as a gift, through the redemption that is in Christ Jesus" (Romans 3:23-24). It is nothing other than the grace of God that saves us. This is good news, friend.

Jesus was crucified to death so that you might have life. Real life.

## CRUCIFIED TO LIFE

The work of Jesus didn't stop at the cross. God raised Jesus to life on the third day, stamping His approval on Jesus' work and affirming everything that Jesus said about Himself. Jesus didn't just get crucified on a cross and stay in the tomb; He rose to life just as He said He would do. Countless times He told His followers that He would have to suffer and would be raised on the third day (Luke 9:22).

If Christ was not raised from the dead, our faith would be in vain – at least that is what the Apostle Paul told the church in Corinth. It was by the Spirit of God that Christ was raised, and this same Spirit is the gift given to His followers today. That's right. The same Spirit who raised Jesus from the dead is the same Spirit who lives inside of us. The Spirit of God has been given to us so that our lives may be filled with abundance – so that we can do greater things than Jesus did (read John 14:12).

## CRUCIFIED FOR YOU

Too many self-professing Christians lack an understanding of grace. Too many people are going through each day with a deep-seated doubt in their mind of whether they are truly forgiven or not. If only we could get this one thing right. If only we would lower the walls we have created so that we can receive grace.

Focusing this much on grace isn't just about giving you more theology. It's not about giving you more creeds. It's about giving you what God has already offered you: life. It's about showing you the reality of the depths and vastness of God's love for you.

Grace is the great stumbling block for mankind. It is counterintuitive. It goes against everything we know, and everything we grew up believing. Grace doesn't make sense. It's an absolute ridiculous answer to the huge problem mankind finds itself in. All people have wronged the Creator of the Universe and this demands punishment. But God is not setting out to meet your expectations, He is setting out to destroy your expectations. God is about showing you more than you can even comprehend.

## A Homeless Shelter, A Muslim, and Me

It lasted for about three hours. It was one of the most philosophical and theological conversations I have ever had. Randall, the gentleman who I had the privilege of speaking with for this long, was the most intellectual twenty-year-old I had ever met. He thought a lot about his faith and his commitment to it. He had quite a personal story as well.

He grew up in Texas. He didn't have a High School diploma, but he was working on getting his GED. He was staying at a homeless shelter because he didn't have anywhere else to go. I believe, though, that the future will be bright for him. We talked and talked and talked. I thoroughly enjoyed our conversation, but I walked away sad.

Randall talked about Jesus. He talked about God. He talked about Mohammad. I listened. I knew that if I just listened long enough I would eventually know what to say to this young man. He was so focused on becoming a better person. He was driven, smart, and a deep thinker.

Little by little I took the opportunity to ask a question here and a question there. I was trying to lead him to what I thought would be his stumbling block. For Muslims and all other religions in the world, salvation is dependent upon good works. In the system of Islam, a person can strive to be the best he or she can be, yet in the end, it is all up to Allah to have mercy. No guarantees. No assurance. Nothing.

This motivation – this desire – is an honorable one to say the least. For someone to stay so committed to his or her faith despite the lack of assurance of salvation is amazing to me. As honorable and *nice* as this way of life is, it's problematic.

After hours of listening and asking questions I took the opportunity to share God's grace with Randall. I was so excited to finally get to the gift that was available to this young man. My blood was pumping extra hard. My adrenaline was flowing. I was so excited for Randall to come to faith in Jesus and to see Him become a follower of Christ. I was pumped.

If only that is how it worked out. Randall legitimately did not understand grace. It was a major stumbling block to him. Grace is a stumbling block to all who place their hope in their own goodness.

## Christian Muslims

As odd as it sounds, this world is full of Christian Muslims. In other words, this world is full of people who confess Christ and live as if they are confessing Mohammed. They sing about Jesus, yet wonder if the words they sing are true. They pray to Jesus, yet they think they need to constantly ask for forgiveness. Christian Muslims are present predominantly in the American Church. I know this because I witness it. I hear the way American Christians talk. They are more interested in behavior modification in themselves, and certainly in others, than they are about intimately knowing Christ. This is because their morality determines their eternal destination, or so they think. But, they couldn't be more wrong.

It breaks my heart when someone doesn't understand grace. I want nothing more than to sit down with him or her and talk about grace until he or she gets it. Like Randall, though, most people have walls up, pushing grace out, to which I want nothing more than a demolition day.

It is so easy for the people in our churches to miss grace. When all pastors want to talk about is morality, what should we expect? Too many professing Christians are living as if they are unsure of their salvation. This is *the* biggest problem in modern Christianity.

In our valiant, unwavering effort of fighting the *culture wars*, we have entirely missed the point of our faith. Instead of preaching hope, American Christianity has been preaching truth without grace. And truth without grace isn't truth at all.

Grace is the good news of Jesus and it cannot be ignored. Grace is what took Christ to the cross.

## Real Christian Hope

The grace of God confronts everything in our being. It pierces deep within, cutting through the skin, slicing through the bone, and ultimately taking up residence in our hearts. It flies in the face of the way we parent our kids. It fundamentally changes the way we think about ourselves.

We may struggle with self-image. We may question whether we are valued. We may seek out everyone's opinions – many people do. Girls seek out the eyes of guys and guys seek out the adoration of girls - both in a desperate ploy to be valued by someone, anyone. I can tell when people are confronted with the grace of God because everything in them begins to get jumbled. Their perspective toward themselves changes. Their outlook on life is radically changed. They finally begin seeing right side up, for they've been upside down for too long.

It can't be overstated: grace is the exact opposite of what we deserve. We absolutely don't deserve it; we deserve nothing except judgment. Thank God that He is who He is! When everything in us tells us that we are unworthy, He is telling us that He loves us anyway.

The grace of God is like a hurricane, destroying the idea that our good works count for something. It took Jesus coming to earth as a willing sacrifice for us to be put into a right relationship with God. There is absolutely nothing that we can do to earn this; it is a gift.

That gift is for you. No matter what you have done, no matter who you think you are, no matter what other people say about you, the gift is for you. You don't have to hope in your behavior; you can hope in your Savior. When your behavior wavers, your Savior stays the same. The actions of Jesus tell me that He absolutely adores you. God looks upon you with the eyes of a loving Father who desires the best for you. He embraces you despite your brokenness, despite your past, and despite your present. He embraces you because He loves you. His embrace is powerful yet gentle, and the crazy thing is, He won't let go. "For I am sure that neither death nor life, nor angels nor rulers, nor things present nor things to come, nor powers, [39] nor height nor depth, nor anything else in all creation, will be able to separate us from the love of God in Christ Jesus our Lord" (Romans 8:38-39). Paul's words are powerful. There is no one and no thing that can separate us from the embrace, the love, and the grace of God. Let that truth linger. Don't brush past it. The great Creator of the Universe, the All in All, the Alpha and the Omega, Yahweh, God, loves you.

It's time that we abandon our hope in our behavior and completely trust in Christ. It's time that we stop being Christian Muslims. Jesus offers something infinitely greater than some religious system. He offers grace. He offers life. He offers Himself. No longer do we need to picture ourselves striving to find God; we can picture God coming down and finding us, for that is what has happened. While we were running from Him, He was running after us. That's right. Not only does Jesus offer Himself for us, but He also runs after us, calling us to Himself.

The Christian hope is that no matter what your past is, and no matter what your present is, you can come to

Jesus just as you are and He will accept you and begin to change you from the inside out. Everyone is invited to come to Jesus. You're not the exception to this; he is calling you to come to Him. He has wrapped the gift up for you, waiting to give it to you. Will you come to Him and receive it?

## A Missing Button

My oldest daughter loves her books. It's quite adorable to see her walk over to her bookshelf, grab a book, bring it to me, and sit on my lap. I enjoy reading to her even though she rarely lets me finish the story before she is on to the next book. There was one day, though, that was different. She brought me the book *Corduroy* and, being in a rather hyper mood, I proceeded to read the book in a highly animated way. She was engaged with the book and so was I. Though, while I was reading to her, I found something very surprising.

If you're not familiar with *Corduroy*, let me fill you in. The story begins at a toy store where a little teddy bear named Corduroy is hoping that today will be the day that he gets to go to a home. A mother and daughter are introduced into the story. The daughter wants to get Corduroy, but her mom doesn't let her. She says no for a couple of reasons: she doesn't have the money and Corduroy wasn't in good condition. He had a button missing and that made the mom fail to see the value in Corduroy.

Corduroy didn't realize he was missing a button so he spends that whole night trying to find it. He is unsuccessful, though. The next day, the little girl who was at the toy store the day before comes in as soon as the store opens. She had gathered up all her money the previous night and is now able to purchase Corduroy. And when she gets him home, she fixes his missing button. The girl is ecstatic to have her Corduroy and Corduroy is ecstatic to finally have a home - a place where he could be loved.

So, what's the surprising thing I found in the story?

Corduroy is a message about grace!

As I read that book to my little girl, I couldn't help but think about how much alike we all are to Corduroy. We all have a button or two missing. We are not perfect; we are quite broken, in fact. We have times where we are not so desirable. Often, we feel out of place and many of us don't have a place we can call home. We may have a place to stay, but a home? That is something we deeply desire. Corduroy desired a home - a place where he could be loved. And he found it.

The little girl saw something in Corduroy that many people didn't: she saw the value in him despite his brokenness. While Corduroy spent all night trying to find his missing button so that he could fix himself, the girl spent all night gathering her money so that she could purchase him. Dare I say that the little girl reminds me of what Jesus did for us? You bet I do.

Jesus purchased us with His blood. Even though we have some buttons missing, He loves us anyway and paid the price that had to be paid for us to be in a relationship with God.

It doesn't stop there. It gets better. The little girl brought Corduroy home after she bought him. She fixed his missing button. She put him back together. The Holy Spirit does the same thing to us. He takes the brokenness in our lives and transforms us into who we are supposed to be. If we think we can put ourselves back together on our own, we are kidding ourselves. We are made new only by the grace of God. God takes us while we are messed up and He loves us anyway. "God shows his love for us in that while we were still sinners, Christ died for us." (Romans 5:8). That's the beauty of grace.

## AWE-STRUCK

If the reality of God's grace doesn't bring you to your knees in heartfelt worship, I don't know what will. While we were enemies of God, God sent Jesus so that we can be called His friend. Deeper than that, God calls us His children. From enemies to children, God's grace reconciles sinners to Himself and Himself to sinners.

You are loved. I can't say it enough. In Christ, you are forgiven, redeemed, reconciled, and justified. Let us enjoy this reality. Let us thank God for what He has done. Let us worship Him for the amazing God that He is.

At the beginning of this chapter I asked you this question: what do you think about when you think about what God thinks about you? Consider this question again. My prayer is that your answer has changed if it needed to. My prayer is that you see that God loves you, likes you, values you, adores you, and cares deeply for you.

One of the most intriguing statements Jesus spoke when He was here on earth is this: "The thief comes only to steal and kill and destroy. I came that they may have life and have it abundantly" (John 10:10). Contrasting His mission with the enemy's mission, Jesus says that He has come so that they, as in you and me, may have abundant life. What does it mean to live an abundant life? That's the focus for the rest of this book.

Would you join me on this journey to abundant life? I pray that you will.

# CHAPTER 2

# THE CALL TO YOU

*23 And he said to all, "If anyone would come after me, let him deny himself and take up his cross daily and follow me. 24 For whoever would save his life will lose it, but whoever loses his life for my sake will save it. 25 For what does it profit a man if he gains the whole world and loses or forfeits himself? 26 For whoever is ashamed of me and of my words, of him will the Son of Man be ashamed when he comes in his glory and the glory of the Father and of the holy angels. – Luke 9:23-26*

"God is calling me to go to India." These were the words I heard a man say recently. It was a Thursday night at an Elder's meeting and this pastor, this family man, this Jesus follower was about to take his family and move them across the world for the sake of the Gospel.

He proceeded to tell us how dangerous the area was where he felt God calling them. He explained that India was full of radical Hindus and that they were just as bad as the radical Muslims we see on the news. To be a Christ follower in this part of India was to have a death wish but this didn't deter he and his family from going. I know this because they are there right now as I write these words. They are in this hostile country getting acclimated with the culture, learning the language, building relationships with locals, and training pastors.

Hearing this man talk about what God is calling he and his family to do is humbling because he knows that their calling could cost them their lives. As afraid as they may be, they are there right now in that hostile place, infiltrating the darkness with the light of Jesus.

Their story isn't much different from ours. Sure, we may not have been called to go overseas as missionaries (not yet anyway), but we have been called to deny ourselves. In fact, that is the call that Jesus makes to every single person who desires to follow after Him. This isn't a call for the *super Christians*; it is a call to *every* Christian. No one is exempt from this calling and no one can come up with a reasonable argument that would excuse him or her from it. The call is for the business man, the female executive, the lawyer who is about to make partner, the college student, the accountant, the computer programmer, the sports coach, the band director, the platinum recording artist, the stay-at-home mom, the stay-at-home dad, the busy, the bored, the overwhelmed, the extrovert, the introvert, and everyone in-between. The call is for me, and the call is for you.

## THE CALL TO DIE

*When Christ calls a man, he bids him come and die. — Dietrich Bonhoeffer*

Anyone who desires to follow Jesus is confronted by His radical words. Jesus is not interested in mere intellectual belief; the price He paid was for something much more. Jesus paid our debt with His very life, thus for us to come after Him requires our very lives. This has been lost in American Christianity. God is not calling us to a comfortable and cozy faith, but rather a radical losing of our lives daily as we follow Jesus.

There is a cost to following Jesus, the Son of God who came to set us free from this world, from ourselves, from our comfort, from our boredom, and from our insignificance. That cost is our life. Jesus, knowing the radical nature of His call, told the people to count the cost. He told them that wise builders count the cost before they begin their project because it would be pointless to begin just to have to stop later, realizing that the cost was too great (Luke 14:28).

Jesus tells every person who desires to come after Him, "let him deny himself and take up his cross daily and follow me" (Luke 9:23). The people who first heard Jesus' words knew exactly what He was calling them to do when He said to take up their cross. To follow Jesus was to do the unthinkable – to willingly take up a Roman cross and walk to their death daily. The call to us today is the same.

The effect of Jesus' statement is easily lost in our society. We wear crosses around our necks, we put them on our walls, we have them in our church buildings, we put them on the bumpers of our cars, and rightly so, for it is a symbol of hope for us. This is not how first century people would have understood the cross. And for us to truly understand Jesus' call to us, we must adopt the view of those who lived in the first century.

The Roman Empire was notorious for utilizing tactics that would deter people from rebelling. One of these tactics was to crucify people along the main roads that lead into cities. Imagine taking a family trip to Jerusalem. You're likely walking with many other people – for it was much safer to travel in large groups – and as you approach the city of Jerusalem you are confronted with a stench. The hair in your nose goes stiff as the smell of rotting corpses enters your nasal passage. Whatever joyful anticipation you were experiencing as you approached Jerusalem is gone because you are now overwhelmed by the stench of crucified bodies. The paralyzing smell reaches into your gut, into your heart, and causes your throat to swell up. You are nervous, afraid, wondering whether it is a good idea to continue toward the great city. You begin to wonder, *what did they do?* The world you live in isn't as nice as you thought it was. This is the first time you are confronted with crucified bodies. Broken legs are attached to beaten bodies. The birds have begun to eat away at the corpses. Instead of using anti-crime billboards, the Romans have gotten their message across to you in a far more powerful way. They have warned every sense in your body: you smell their warning, you see it, you feel it, you can taste it in the air, and you can hear the silence. Roman marketers have successfully freaked you out. You will submit to this power because of what they will do to you if you don't.

Having been confronted with the reality of the first century, you are now faced with the words of Jesus. To follow this Rabbi, you are to get one of those crosses and walk with it each day, denying yourself. Physical death isn't out of the question – for Jesus doesn't rule it out – but spiritual death is certainly in order, and He expounds upon it. Deny yourself. This is the way of He who is calling you. Jesus cannot have people of self-interest following Him because that is not going to work with His mission.

*Yeah, I'd love for you to follow me. Your cross is over there.*

A Christian without a cross is not a Christian at all. Jesus demands and requires anyone who desires to follow Him to take up a cross. It's a heavy cross; it weighs a lot, sure. But more than that, it is heavy on the will. Willingly taking up a cross is not what we naturally desire to do. Jesus doesn't care what our desires are in this matter, though, for He tells us to deny ourselves. He knows that if we take up our cross without denying ourselves, we will drop the cross after just a short distance.

## Jesus' Call to a Rich Man

A question we have all asked is *how good do I need to be to get to heaven?* A certain brave young man asked Jesus this question as well. The account can be read in Matthew 19:16-30. This man comes to Jesus asking what good things he must do to inherit eternal life. Jesus responds with a question, like He seems to always do. "And he said to him, 'Why do you ask me about what is good? There is only one who is good. If you want to enter life, keep the commandments'" (v. 17). Obviously showing the rhetorical nature of His own question, Jesus gives the man what he wants: He says to keep the commandments.

The man wants to know which ones in particular. Jesus tells him the biggies like not murdering, not committing adultery, loving your neighbor, etc… Being confident, the man confirms that he has kept them all and asks, "What do I still lack?" (v. 20).

At this point, this confident man has opened himself up for Jesus to cut to the very thing that he has placed his hope in the most. The man probably was a *good person*, by human standards anyway. He probably did the right things, said the right things, gave to the right causes, and was just an overall good person. Maybe you can relate to this man. You may have never murdered anyone. You may have never cheated on your spouse. You probably do your best to be a loving person. You have probably kept these commandments but still wonder, *is there something I am still lacking?*

If only Jesus' response to this man would have been, "Good job, bud, you are saved and good to go!" Instead, Jesus pinpoints the thing that is paramount in this man's life. He tells him, "If you would be perfect, go, sell what you possess and give to the poor, and you will have treasure in heaven; and come, follow me" (v. 21). Cutting to this man's heart, Jesus goes straight to the man's wallet. To see where his allegiance resided, to see if this man was truly willing to deny himself for the sake of Jesus, Jesus tells him to get rid of all that he possesses and will in turn receive treasure in heaven. What a great deal, right?

The man does not respond to Jesus' words with joy. He doesn't jump up and down and thank Him for giving him the promise of treasure in heaven. Upon hearing Jesus' words, the man shifts his gaze away from Jesus and turns it to the ground. His head drops down, his shoulders begin to sag, and he walks away. The man walks away sad because he has great wealth. He has worked hard for what he has and is not about to give it all away because this Rabbi tells him to do so. He is not about to give up something in the present to have more than he could imagine in the future. That apparently isn't a good enough return on investment for the rich man.

## Jesus' Call to the Rich

After the man walks away, Jesus turns to his disciples and says, "Truly, I say to you, only with difficulty will a rich person enter the kingdom of heaven" (v. 23). In other words, it is basically impossible. He gives the word picture that "it is easier for a camel to go through the eye of a needle than for a rich person to enter the kingdom of God" (v. 24). Perplexed by Jesus' teaching, the disciples conclude, *that's impossible, Jesus!* His point is made. Jesus relieves the tension, at least partly, and says that the impossible is possible with God (v. 26).

If we're not careful, we'll gloss over this teaching of Jesus because we don't typically view ourselves in the same category as this rich young man. Here's the reality, though: if you make $25,000 a year, you are in the top 2 percent of the world's wealthiest people.[1] Just $25,000, not one million or even six figures, puts you into the category of "filthy rich." If you live in America and make this amount of money, you probably don't look at yourself as a rich person. Why? Everyone around you, it seems, makes more money than you do. Relatively speaking, you are on the low end of the totem pole in the American economy. You barely make enough to afford a decent apartment and pay for your necessities. You don't *feel* rich, do you? I don't either, but that doesn't change the facts. We *are* in the top 2 percent of the wealthiest of people in this world. There's no debate.

Given our reality, our wealth status, what shall we do in response to Jesus' teaching? No matter what the Spirit leads us to do, we must do it. But in this, I don't want us to miss the point of Jesus' teaching: it is impossible for the rich man to enter the kingdom of heaven. Why is this? I have wrestled with the implications of this passage ever since I first read it, and even more so after realizing that I am coupled into the same category as the rich man.

---

[1] See GlobalRichList.com

What is it about being rich that makes it impossible to enter the kingdom?

Wealth blinds. It blinds people of their need for a Savior. When we have all that we need and much, much more, we typically don't turn to God to provide for our needs. For the poor among us, they have to depend on God for their basic necessities. We just get in one of our cars – most of us have two – and head to the grocery store. The store is lined with choices beyond choices. *What do I want? What do I need?* No matter how we answer those questions, we can satisfy those wants and needs easily. We are rich. We are blinded.

So, what shall we do, we who are rich? Jesus gives us a glimpse in His response to the rich man – give up whatever we are putting ahead of Him – but we'll see Jesus' words to *every* person who desires to follow Him in the next section. Neither the rich nor the poor are exempt from Jesus' words in Luke 9.

## THE CALL TO LIVE

*Submit to death, death of your ambitions and favourite wishes every day and death of your whole body in the end submit with every fibre of your being, and you will find eternal life. Keep back nothing. Nothing that you have not given away will be really yours. Nothing in you that*

*has not died will ever be raised from the dead. Look for*
*yourself, and you will find in the long run only hatred,*
*loneliness, despair, rage, ruin, and decay. But look for*
*Christ and you will find Him, and with Him everything*
*else thrown in. – C.S. Lewis*

"If anyone would come after me, let him deny himself and take up his cross and follow me" (Matthew 16:24). Jesus is brilliant in the way that He expounds upon this radical teaching as He grabs the people's attention, and certainly ours as well, and drills the point even deeper. The key to following Jesus is to take up your cross. As you know, this would have been understood as walking to your death, daily. So, the key to following Jesus thus far is to die in some way. This, though, isn't the end of the story. Jesus goes on to say that "whoever would save his life will lose it, but whoever loses his life for my sake will save it" (Luke 9:24). This isn't the first time that Jesus says something that makes you scratch your head and it won't be the last either. To live an abundant life, you must lose your life. And this means giving up something valuable to us: control.

Jesus knows that our tendency is to control. We desire to be in control of every situation we are involved in. This is no different when it comes to our salvation; we think we need to do this and do that to gain God's favor.

We begin thinking like many of the first-century Jews in Jesus' context. The Pharisees were so committed to upholding God's law that they put rules around the law so that they would be even more insulated from sin. In the process, they became legalistic, dependent upon their own goodness, and ended up missing the Messiah who was directly in front of them.

Jesus also knows that we are screwed if it is up to us to reach salvation. He knows why He came. He knows the implications of His mission. He came to go to the cross, to defeat sin and death, and to rise victoriously so that we have an opportunity to die to the sinful selves that hold us in judgment before a Holy God. The only way a person can find his life is to lose what his life has become – fogged, altered, and cracked from the world. Jesus knows that our lives are not as they are supposed to be. Abundant life, the life Jesus calls His followers to, is a journey of loss that results in gain.

That is why Jesus came: to call His followers to get rid of their old selves so that they may be made new. The transformation, however, is attributable only to God.

## The Driven Person and Jesus

I have a problem. My problem isn't something that the world recognizes, for the world looks at it and rejoices. I am a driven person. Give me something to do, give me some cause to fight for, give me a purpose, and I will go achieve.

From my first experience of sports and competition, it was clear that I was driven to win, to achieve. I can remember my family asking me after basketball games, baseball games, and hockey games, "Did you have fun?" They were concerned because my face during the games was like stone. I looked mad. I looked intense. They were worried. I can remember looking at them dumbfounded. *Of course, I had fun*, I thought. And that is what I would say to them. *Of course, I had fun – I was playing sports. Duh!* My family quickly learned that during sports and other forms of competition, I turned into a stone-faced, determined, and driven-to-win person.

I hate to lose. I love to win. I love to achieve. I love to accomplish. I have a problem. I tend to want to gain more and more than what I currently have. Before I was in full-time ministry, I was in a sales environment. I loved sales. I loved it because it gave me an outlet for incentive-based achievements. I have a problem.

Jesus looks to you and He looks to me and asks, "What good is it for a man to gain the whole world, and yet lose or forfeit his very self?" (Luke 9:25). In my deep desire to win, I lose. I am not just losing some game; I am losing my very soul. By always trying to accomplish, by always trying to gain power, I forfeit myself. Oh, the irony!

In our efforts to do more, we find that the more we do or gain in this world, the more we lose and thus, the more we lose our very souls. This is the way it works in the kingdom of God. The kingdom of God works in opposition of the world. Everything in us tells us to work as hard as we possibly can to gain influence in this world. But, if we continue trying to accomplish and achieve, we'll always be in a losing endeavor – we'll always be searching. In our effort of trying to find ourselves, we'll grow faint because no matter what we find, it won't be what we're truly looking for. This is why we must lose our lives to find them. This is why we must deny ourselves by taking up our cross daily.

## A Proper Posture

The key to understanding what Jesus is calling His followers to in Luke 9 is to understand the posture of faith. When we are brought before the Holy God and we truly realize who He is and who we are, our only reaction should be to fall to our knees. The proper posture before God is a posture of submission and surrender.

Too often the "posture" that people take before God is one where they view God as a nice add-on to their already figured-out lives. Sure, they believe that God exists, but they don't adopt the true posture of faith before Him. Why? They don't seem to understand who God rightly is, for if they knew Him, they would fall at His feet. If they knew Him, they wouldn't be able to help but worship Him. If they knew Him, they would instantly realize that they are unworthy to be in His presence. If they knew Him, they would realize that their half-hearted belief is inadequate. If they knew Him, they would be confronted with Jesus' call to lose their lives.

The proper posture before God is to bow down, worshiping Him and giving up our lives – everything in it, holding nothing back. The result of this? Our lives will be saved. This is a daily endeavor. Jesus knows that if we take up our cross just one day, it won't be enough because it is so easy for us to fall back into depending on our own efforts for salvation. Every single day is a new opportunity to take up our cross, to die to ourselves, so that we may truly live. This is what Jesus wants for you: true life. He knows what needs to happen for you to be able to live that life. You must follow His calling. You must answer it. You must surrender.

The God you are losing your life for is the source life itself. His desire is to give you abundant life. The only thing is, that life may not be what you thought it would look like. It may look like doing the very thing you said you would never do. It's funny hearing people talk about how they said they would *never* do something only to find themselves doing that *very* thing later. God has a funny way of keeping us on our toes, pushing us further than we thought we could go.

Jesus' call has many implications for everyday life. To answer Him when He calls is to lose yourself again. The things that He will call you to will be things of self-emptying, self-sacrifice, and love. The pastor who was called to India knows this very well. He is now a missionary in a hostile environment. Left up to him, without the call of Christ, I'm sure he would have chosen to stay in America. But, that is not the life he chose. He chose the way of the cross, the life that is modeled by following Jesus, and since Jesus took up His cross, this missionary must take up his cross as well. Jesus called this man and his family to be a light in deep darkness. To not follow this call would be to deny Jesus Christ and to attempt to save his own life. In following this call to India, he is truly living.

## BOOT CAMP

My best friend, Tim, is an Army veteran and as I was talking to him about this chapter, I thought to myself that soldiers know exactly what 'deny yourself' means. Before soldiers are ready for battle, the military must break them down and build them back up. In a way, this is similar to what Jesus is calling us to. He is calling us to lose ourselves in Him by denying ourselves every single day, taking up our cross and following Him.

I had a hunch that Tim knew what it was like to have this happen in a unique way because he had experienced it during boot camp. So instead of assuming, I asked him.

On his way to boot camp, he experienced a high level of anticipation. He talked about being on a bus with his fellow Army prospects. When they got to the Reception Battalion, everything started. The drill sergeants boarded the bus and the screaming began. Once off the bus, they were told to take all their belongings and empty them into a box. They were then taken to clothing where they would all change out of their civilian clothes and into their itchy Army sweats.

Tim was starting to feel what it's like to deny himself. They spent two weeks at Reception, getting shots, physicals, and documentation. He quickly found out that those two weeks at Reception were the easiest two weeks of his training. After this, the training was intensified and the denial of self was raised up a few notches.

The most intense time of self-denial for Tim was during a 15-mile-long ruck march when he was carrying 40 pounds of equipment on his back. He talked about the mind games the march played inside his head. Every step required another denial – a denial of the desire to stop going.

It was through this experience that Tim realized how beneficial it was as a soldier to deny himself during his training. He was pushed past where he felt his limits were. He did more than he ever thought he could do because he denied himself and trusted that his drill sergeants knew what they were doing. Tim graduated from Army Basic Training as the top soldier out of 850 others. He was in the top 10% of all people who go through Army Basic Training. The following words capture his experience in a powerful way: "I let who I was go and what people said about me dissolve; I denied who I was and accepted what I needed to do – what I needed to become."

Tim's individual will was destroyed so that his will could be joined together with his fellow soldiers. The military does this to their soldiers so that they know their soldiers will be on the same page. They do this so that every soldier will look out for those who are on their left and on their right.

It was through denying himself that Tim received a new life as a soldier. In a similar way, it is through denying yourself that you are given true, abundant life in Christ.

## WILL YOU ANSWER?

Jesus is calling you to die to yourself so you may experience what real life is – to live as He lived. The question is, *will you answer the call?* Will you decide that life with Christ is better than life without Him? Will you decide that He is the only thing you will live for? Will you decide that answering His call is the most important decision you will ever make?

Jesus promised that if you deny yourself, you will find true life. Will you continue trying to save your life on your own or give up your life for Him? The choice is yours. Jesus is waiting.

CHAPTER 3

# SOMETHING BRAND NEW

*And I will give you a new heart, and a new spirit I will put within you. And I will remove the heart of stone from your flesh and give you a heart of flesh. – Ezekiel 36:26*

Jesus didn't come to offer a new religion. He didn't come to give a political ideology. He didn't come to support the Constitution, to uphold gun rights, or to offer a name-it-claim-it get-rich-quick scheme. He came to bring something brand new. While so many people are stuck in the old way of doing things, the way of law, Jesus proclaims something different. What He came to bring is something unlike anything the world has ever seen.

Jesus came to confront religion directly in the face. While Islam preaches salvation by your own goodness, while Buddhism and Hinduism preach incarnation until perfection, while Judaism preaches hardly anything anymore, while Atheism preaches *God is dead*, and while New Age-ism preaches anything and everything, Jesus preaches hope for the hopeless, healing for the hurting, and life for the dead. His message is superior to all others. Their messages are that of *I hope I'm saved, better luck next time, I don't know anymore, I'm sure there's no hope,* and *whatever works*. It's sad. It's unfortunate. It's heartbreaking because there is a better message. Jesus totally flips the script on religion, turning everything on its head, confronting us with a message of repentance and total surrender. And the best part is, He has the power to deliver!

When every religious opinion is to do better, to keep doing everything you can, and to hope that God isn't mad at you when you die, Jesus is saying *without me you're screwed, but with me you're forgiven, and I'm right there with you*. Jesus is the Rescuer. Yes, Jesus is the Crucified God who came to save us from the pits of Hell, for that is where we were headed. He nailed our wrongs to the cross, paid our debt, and now gives us something more. Not only has He brought us into a reconciled relationship with our Creator, but He has also done something so new that no religious system can speak of such a thing. Jesus took our broken lives and hearts and offers brand new replacements.

## CRUCIFIED WITH CHRIST

At the onset of his letter to the church in Galatia, Paul confronts the Galatians about turning away from the Gospel and toward a different message. They were resorting back to their roots – focusing on doing better and on being the chosen people of God simply because of their bloodline. They were experiencing hardship and realized that they could make it stop if they went back to their old ways. Christianity, if you are unaware, was heavily persecuted in its first 300, or so, years of existence. And this was true for this group in Galatia during the first Century.

Normally Paul writes an extended greeting in his letters to churches, however in this letter, he gets straight to the point. Galatians 1:6 reads, "I am astonished…" He was rather upset with the fact that they were forsaking the true Gospel for something less. The Good News, as he explains to them, is that Jesus changes everything including their very selves. They were deserting the best thing that had ever happened to them.

He begins his explanation by telling his own story. He was a zealous Jew who advanced the ranks of the religion, who persecuted Christians, and who "defended God" against the "blasphemers" who followed Jesus of Nazareth. Paul has a *but* in his story, though. Jesus has a way of doing that – putting *buts* in our stories. He was one thing, BUT then he met Jesus and everything changed. Just look at Paul's words: "so extremely zealous was I for the traditions of my fathers. But when he who had set me apart before I was born, and who called me by his grace, was pleased to reveal his Son to me," everything changed (Galatians 1:14b-16a). Paul then makes the point that the message he preached to the Galatians is one that came straight from God, for he didn't consult with any person after Jesus was revealed to him (read Galatians 1:16b).

Paul's story was so great that when Christians heard about it, they glorified God. Think about this: a persecutor and participator in the murders of those who followed Jesus, was now a messenger of Jesus. That is quite a life change. Jesus brought into this world something brand new and He continues to do this every time a sinner wakes up and devotes his or her life to God in faith.

Paul understands what happened to him. He drives his point home with the people of Galatia, who want to go back to Judaism, by saying, "For through the law I died to the law, so that I might live to God" (Galatians 2:19). He is proclaiming that he had to actually die to the law in order to live to God. Do you see the pattern here? Jesus says that we must lose our life to find it, and Paul is saying that he has *died* to the law and that it took dying for him to live to God. He further explains his spiritual reality when he says, "I have been crucified with Christ. It is no longer I who live, but Christ who lives in me. And the life I now live in the flesh I live by faith in the Son of God, who loved me and gave himself for me" (Galatians 2:20). This reality is not just for Paul; it is for all who come to Christ in faith. Jesus' call is to come and die, to take up the cross daily. Paul's reality is the result of answering Jesus' call. He has been crucified with his Lord; he died to what he used to be. It is in the crucifixion that the "but" is brought into our story. Paul used to live *for* God as a Jew, BUT, now Christ lives *in* him. What an amazing reality!

While the Galatian Christians desire to go back to their Jewish faith in response to the trials of the Christian life, Paul declares that it is impossible to do so, for he (and they) died to that way of life. What are you contemplating on going back to? We all have skeletons in our closets. We all have things in our past that can so easily creep back into our lives if we're not careful. The reality that you live in now, though, is that you died to that way of life. You died to the old you and now, Christ lives in you.

Have you had your "but" moment? Jesus put a huge "but" in Paul's story and He'll do the same to yours. I think Sir Mix-A-Lot was close with his famous song *Baby Got Back*. He likes "big butts," but could it be that there's a better "big but" in life – the one where Jesus declares, *you were once one thing, but that is not who you are any longer?* It's an odd comparison, I know. We will not remix that song into some Christianized version – that would be pitiful – but the comparison works. The old you is gone. No longer shall you define yourself with the same words you used to.

Addict. Not anymore.

Failure. No.

Orphan. No longer.

Unloved. Certainly not.

What term has always defined you? How do others describe you? What is your *word?* What is that dreaded adjective that sucks the life from you? What is your biggest regret? What word do you associate with that? I want you to do something brave – I know it will be hard and I know you probably won't want to, but you need to do this: write down every negative adjective that comes to mind as you think about yourself. These can be words that other people have used to define you as well as words you have used to define yourself. Now that you have been honest, I want you to look at each word you wrote down and draw a line through each word, for you have been crucified with Christ. It is no longer you who live, but Christ lives in you! After you have done that, take a few minutes to pray, thanking God for the gift of a spiritual crucifixion and the presence of Christ in your life.

## JOINING JESUS

Jesus' power is revealed in His willingness to embrace weakness. He was born to die. He came to this earth with His mission in front of him, focused and resolved to see it come to fruition. Nothing was going to stop him. He accomplished His assignment by taking the form of a servant, willingly giving Himself for you and for me. By freely dying on the cross of Calvary and rising from the dead on the third day, Jesus opened the door for us to join Him in something truly amazing: a promise of victory.

The promise is for the whole world – for drug dealers, drug addicts, prostitutes, porn stars, porn addicts, gang bangers, money launderers, minimum-wage workers, social workers, lawyers, entrepreneurs, business executives, inmates, the poor, the rich, and you. The promise is for every single person on this earth. And that promise is this: by coming to Jesus in faith, giving up your whole life, you get to participate in His death and resurrection. Now, that may not be all too exciting unless you understand the implications of such a promise.

In the book of Romans, Paul explains this promise. He is making the case that those who put their faith in

Jesus Christ are justified only by the grace of God – as manifested in the sacrifice of Jesus. He is addressing a group of people inside the Roman church who have decided that because God's grace is so good, they should continue to intentionally sin so that in their sin, they can bring more glory to God. Now, before you write these people off as idiots, think about their reasoning. If the Christian faith consists of salvation being given by God despite your sin, then you can openly sin without affecting your salvation. Responding to this, Paul declares:

> What shall we say then? Are we to continue in sin that grace may abound? [2] By no means! How can we who died to sin still live in it? [3] Do you not know that all of us who have been baptized into Christ Jesus were baptized into his death? [4] We were buried therefore with him by baptism into death, in order that, just as Christ was raised from the dead by the glory of the Father, we too might walk in newness of life.
>
> [5] For if we have been united with him in a death like his, we shall certainly be united with him in a resurrection like his. [6] We know that our old self was crucified with him in order that the body of sin might be brought to nothing, so that we would no longer be enslaved to sin. [7] For one who has died has been set

free from sin. [8] Now if we have died with Christ, we believe that we will also live with him. – Romans 6:1-8

*How can we who died to sin still live in it?* To continue to sin is to go against our new reality. We have surely died to the power that used to hold us in bondage. We do not live the old life that was plagued by all kinds of sin. No! We have died to sin. That sin-ridden person no longer exists.

*Do you not know that all of us who have been baptized into Christ Jesus were baptized into His death?* This is what Paul plainly says. You have joined Jesus in His death so that you may no longer live in sin. Not only is the undesirable washed away, but you have also joined Jesus in His resurrection. You have been given a new life – a second chance, if you will. You have been regenerated and are no longer who you used to be. You are still you, but a better you. In fact, it is in this that you became who you were truly meant to be, who God intended for you to be, for you are now a person who is unhindered in his or her relationship with God.

*Our old self was crucified…* Paul is again declaring that we have been crucified with Christ. The purpose in this is two-fold: you were crucified to have your old self killed and your new self made alive. The following is a truth you should always remember: the best you is the crucified you.

Your crucifixion happened so that you would now be unhindered in clinging completely to our Lord and Savior, Jesus Christ. He is the source of your death and the source of your life. He gives you the blessing of the cross and the blessing of the abundant life. The best you is the crucified you because, in being crucified, you are able to truly live. What used to hold you in bondage has now lost its grip. You used to be a prisoner to sin, yet God's grace has freed you. Your new life of freedom is indebted to the cross of Christ and the radical love in which He poured out on you.

*If we have died with Christ…* The paradox of the Christian hope is that there is life in death – that death precedes life. This is completely backwards from the way the natural world works. Let us not be confused, though. The death where we die with Christ is a victorious death, for in it death is defeated because of the life that follows. This is what Christ's death is all about: defeating death itself. This is what we get to take part in. The resurrection of Jesus is God putting His exclamation point on the death of Jesus, and the same is true for those who decide to follow Jesus. The life they now live is a life of abundance because of the exclamation point of Jesus.

The question we must ask ourselves is this: *am I truly living into my reality?* If the old me has been put to death and the new me is fully alive, then why am I going back to the things I used to do? Am I ignoring what has happened to me? I'm not talking about reaching perfection, I'm simply talking about living into our new life, for it is not us who live, but Christ who lives in us. Do you believe that?

You have power over the sin that used to rule your world. You may not win every battle, but because of what Jesus has done, you'll win the war. The battle is going to be a struggle, I promise. Take a moment to think of some of your biggest sins – those things that continue to creep into your life. Are you putting up any resistance? We tend to call our sins our struggles, but a struggle necessitates a fight. Are you fighting? Keep in mind, you are not fighting the battle alone. You've been prepared for victory and, ultimately, you've already been given the victory. It's now just a matter of walking into that victory, but it will take a fight. Are you going to fight? You died to the old you and now you get to live as the best you, the crucified you. Jesus didn't just defeat death and sin so that you would be forgiven; He also defeated death so that you could join Him in His death, and furthermore, so that you could join Him in His life – the abundant life.

## A SIMPLE EQUATION

I used to love math. Please take special notice of the past tense: I *used* to love math. I loved it when I was good at it.

I looked at math as one of my best subjects in school. In elementary school, I did well in math. In middle school, I did well in math (except for one semester where I didn't do any homework at all – this was my *cool* stage). In high school, I did well in math. I loved trigonometry. I loved algebra. I put up with geometry. When I decided to switch my major to start my sophomore year of college from criminology to computer science, I was confronted with something frightening: calculus.

I thoroughly did not enjoy calculus because I just didn't get it. My professor was so good at math that he sped through every problem on the board with lightning speed. As I tried to copy down the second step of a problem, he moved on to the next problem. Sometimes, just because you're good at something doesn't mean you should be a teacher of the thing you're good at – but that's a conversation for a different time. I was discouraged because calculus didn't make much sense to me. It was complicated and I lacked the motivation to teach myself what I needed to know.

Luckily, the economy of the Kingdom of God is not as complicated. In fact, the equation I am going to give you may be the simplest of equations you've ever encountered. It's an equation that is put in place only by the wisdom and grace of God.

Here it is: In Christ + Nothing = New Creation

Paul writes, "Therefore, if anyone is in Christ, he is a new creation. The old has passed away; behold, the new has come. All this is from God, who through Christ reconciled us to himself and gave us the ministry of reconciliation" (2 Corinthians 5:17-18). These two verses get to the heart of what it means to be a Christian. For those who are in Christ, newness has come and what was old has passed away. The old you is gone because something better has come.

In order to be created anew in Christ, you must first die to the old you. This is made possible through the cross of Christ. Jesus takes your sin and nails it to the cross. In your own spiritual crucifixion, you are walking into your new reality. You have been made new even if you don't look like it yet, for spiritual maturity is a process. The reality is, whether you realize it yet or not, is that you have been made new in Christ and have been reconciled to God.

Imagine the following scenario. Two people are in the middle of a dispute that has been going on for too long. Realizing that it will only get worse if they continue, one of them proposes that they bring in a third party to act as a mediator. The other concurs, as they are both at a loss for a solution that they will both agree to.

Now picture yourself sitting at a table where your Heavenly Father is sitting across from you. Just imagine the scene in your mind. Better yet, take the scene to your own dining room table, or the table you usually eat at – you on one side and your Heavenly Father on the other. The two of you are in a dispute and finding a solution that accomplishes the goal seems to be out of the question and impossible to find. God wants you to be reconciled to Himself, but you have sinned against Him. Being the perfect and holy God that He is, He will not just brush your sin away and ignore it. You want forgiveness and He wants to give you forgiveness, but someone must pay for the wrong that has been done by you.

Enter the mediator. Jesus, the Son of God, joins the dinner table. His assignment is to bring about reconciliation to the situation. He is there to act as a third party, to bring about a new angle that neither of you have thought of. In His love and wisdom, He volunteers to be the One to bring about reconciliation by taking on your punishment. This is a picture of what has happened. For Jesus, the mediator between you and the Father, has taken on your punishment so that you can get what you don't deserve: forgiveness.

Now this is not to paint the picture that the Father didn't already have this planned. He knew how mankind would be redeemed and reconciled to Himself before He even created us. It was in His divine wisdom that He sent the Son to be the atoning sacrifice for us, the sacrifice that took on His wrath that was due us.

In a dispute with your Creator, you were. In a loving relationship with your Creator, you are. You are a new creation; you are one who is reconciled to a former enemy, for you made God your enemy when you took hold of sin. Yet in His love for you, God brought about reconciliation to your relationship with Him. This is all the work of God; you don't get to take any credit for it – you did nothing. That which needed to be done has been done by the only One who could do it: Jesus Christ. All your sin – every bit of it from your past, present, and future – was nailed to the cross.

You see, it all comes together beautifully. When you lose your life for God, you lose that which was old, that which was undesirable, that which was in sin. What you are given is something brand new, a new you, a new life. And this is why the crucified you is the best you. For the crucified you is brand new. The crucified you is the reconciled you. The crucified you is the forgiven you. Do you see it? The abundant life that Jesus came to give you is found in the death of the old you. Abundant life comes when the old you ceases to breathe and the new you comes to life.

## Abundant Labels

I absolutely loved high school. When I reflect on that fact around other people, though, I find that many people don't share that sentiment. Let's be honest, for many people, high school was hell. It was a place full of labels, and if you were on the wrong end of them, you were miserable. Teenagers can be quite brutal. In most cases, I was on the positive side of these labels. I wasn't labeled a nerd, a jerk (maybe I was by some), an idiot, white trash, or anything else. I played lots of sports, got decent grades, and hung out with the *cool* kids. I absolutely loved high school.

Drama. It's some people's middle name. Over the years, I've learned that it is best to avoid drama. Being in vocational ministry, though, I can't exactly run from it. But in high school, I avoided it as best as I could because I knew that there was always pain with drama. There is pain in labels too and I'm afraid that you may have received a negative label at some point in your life.

Whore. Failure. Stupid. Hot head. Low life.

What's your label? What has someone called you that stuck and that haunts you when you least expect it? I have good news for you. The ones who have labeled you do not have the authority to label you. There is only One who has the right to label you and His name is Jesus. He has bought you with a great price: His very life. He has the right to label you and He has flipped the script on your past labels. He has redeemed you, friend!

*I'm just a sinner saved by grace...* In one sense, you are correct, but in another sense, you are completely wrong. If you've been in the church for long, you know that 'sinner' is a label you have been given. At some point a pastor has probably preached on Romans 3:23, "for all have sinned and fall short of the glory of God," and I am willing to bet that he left out Romans 3:24 which says, "and are justified by his grace as a gift, through the redemption that is in Christ Jesus." You see, the story doesn't end with sin; it ends with Christ Jesus. Furthermore, the story doesn't end with your failure; it ends with the victory of Christ – it ends with knowing that He has brought redemption to your whole life.

It is because of your redemption that Jesus has ripped off the label 'sinner' and has replaced it with 'saint.' The label 'saint' isn't only reserved for Mother Theresa and Francis of Assisi; it is given to you and all who follow Jesus. So, go ahead and tell your friends to begin calling you saint _____, for the One who has the right to label you has redeemed you, and He has declared that you are a saint.

Don't believe me? Consider that when Paul begins and ends his letters, he says things like, "Greet every saint in Christ Jesus. The brothers who are with me greet you"

(Philippians 4:21). Why would Paul say to greet every saint if the only saints were people like Francis of Assissi and Mother Theresa? As odd as it sounds, and as weird as it may feel, you are a saint. You are a saint, not because of something great you did for God, but because of the amazing thing He has done for you through the death of Jesus Christ, your Lord and Savior.

Jesus has the power to redeem you no matter what you have done, no matter your labels. Nothing is beyond His grasp. You're not beyond His grasp. The person down the street isn't beyond His grasp. Your coworkers aren't beyond His grasp. Jesus turns hellions into holy ones. He takes the hell in you and purges it out, for you are crucified with Him. Your sinful life has been done away with and you have been given a new life – a holy life. It is Christ who lives in you and it is for this reason that you can confidently be called 'holy.' What Jesus has done was pay the payment you deserved to pay. He has wiped your account clean and you are now set apart from the rest of the world as someone who is right with God.

Struggle with anger and rage? Know that the old you has been crucified and you have been given new life. You have been given the Holy Spirit to live inside of you, to work through you, to guide you, to comfort you, to point you to Christ. The Holy Spirit working inside of you is what makes you able to be called 'righteous' over 'enraged.' You have a life-giving label now.

There is one label exchange that is utterly crazy. It displays the relentless love of Christ, the crazy grace of the Father, and the hope of the Christian life. Before Christ, you were an *enemy* of God. With Christ, you are counted as a *friend* of God. Jesus says it plainly to His disciples: "No longer do I call you servants, for the servant does not know what his master is doing; but I have called you friends, for all that I have heard from my Father I have made known to you" (John 15:15). To take it a step further, when Abraham believed God, it was credited it to him as righteousness and "…he was called a friend of God" (James 2:23). Without Jesus, we are all enemies of God. We have no hope and we are at odds with the Creator of the Universe. That is very, very bad news. Paul tells the Christians in Rome the same thing. He says, "For if while we were enemies we were reconciled to God by the death of his Son, much more, now that we are reconciled, shall we be saved by his life" (Romans 5:10). While we were enemies (of God) we were reconciled to Him by the death of His Son. Do you see how big this is? Imagine again the dispute with God, the Creator of the Universe, at your dinner table. The picture you see is the very reality that we all face without Christ. God is love, but He is also holy and upholds His law.

Without Jesus as your source of life and salvation, you are left to law. How great God's grace is that He would send Jesus to rescue you from the results of being an enemy of His!

Perhaps the greatest and most life-giving label exchange is this: Jesus has brought you from 'dead' to 'fully alive.' As profound as it is, this is more than a label exchange, it is a spiritual reality.

> And you, who were dead in your trespasses and the uncircumcision of your flesh, God made alive together with him, having forgiven us all our trespasses, by canceling the record of debt that stood against us with its legal demands. This he set aside, nailing it to the cross. – Colossians 2:13-14

In sin, we were all dead, but God has made us alive *with* Him. He set aside our debt, the debt we couldn't pay, by nailing it to the cross. Our sin has been nailed to the cross. Our dead way of life before Christ has been nailed to the cross. We have been given new life just as we have been given a life-changing death. What happens at the cross of Christ is a life-changing death, for His death makes possible our death. And because He died for me and for you, we get a new life, a fresh start, a life that is full of…life. Abundant life. We participate in Jesus' death and His resurrection, for He brings dead things to life.

Life-giving labels come with abundant life. Jesus bursts onto the scene of our life and rips off those old labels that others have put on us, and He gives us the only true labels we need, for He is the only one with the right to label us in the first place.

## THE BEST YOU

The best you is the crucified you. And the crucified you is indwelled with the very Spirit of God. He enables you to live the abundant life that Jesus came to give you. You have been made completely brand new. You have been crucified with Christ, and it is Christ who lives in you. Since you have died to the old you, you can live as the best you. Because of what Christ has done, you have been completely relabeled and are now completely redefined.

## CHAPTER 4

# A HOLY UNION AND DIVINE PURPOSE

---

*We need never shout across the spaces to an absent God.*
*He is nearer than our own soul, closer than our most*
*secret thoughts. — A.W. Tozer*

The most profound truth in the world is that God came down (and this is where people usually stop with the work of God) and decided that He would dwell within us. To understand the profundity of this truth, I would like to share with you a manifesto of the supremacy and glory of Christ.

### THE SUPREMACY AND GLORY OF CHRIST

How big is the Jesus you worship? Do you worship a Jesus designated to be a seasoning to sprinkle over your life? Is the Jesus you worship found in the medicine cabinet - your last attempt to get rid of your pain and trouble?

## Is He This Big?

The only Jesus who is worthy of our worship, who is worthy to be called Savior, who is worthy to be called Lord, is the Jesus who is God's own Son. The infinite God, greater than words can describe, is seen through Him. In fact, Jesus *is* the image of the invisible, eternal, all-powerful, all-present, all-knowing God. When you look upon *this* Jesus, you see God Himself.

General contractors, architects, designers, and foremen do not compare to Jesus. He started with a blank slate, and what He created is all that we know and all that we don't know. The expansive universe is His creation. He decided one day to create, and what was made is beyond our comprehension. He created the Milky Way galaxy, one of only one hundred billion galaxies (no big deal), with a special idea. He decided to place within this galaxy, you and me – such small pieces to this grand creation, this beautiful canvas, so elaborate, so large, so amazing. The angels look upon what Christ has done amazed at the detail and intentionality; they look upon the great canvas of the universe like hipsters do at art galleries - they are blown away.

It wasn't because of an assignment from the Father that Jesus created all that He did; He did it for Himself. He did it for Himself. He did it because He wanted to. That is correct. He created you because He wanted to. He created you for Himself - nothing more, nothing less. So what's the purpose of your life? Christ.

If Jesus ever decided to loosen His embrace, everything would fall apart. All that we know, every law of physics, all molecules, and all cells would cease to exist. It is because of His embrace that we can have the field of science, for without His embrace, all would be random - no meaning, no purpose, no consistency, nothing to observe. Everything is held together by His embrace. Everything is His. The entire Universe is His painting, His story, His poem, His creative expression, His novel, His movie, His experience, His.

Joined to Jesus is the Church, a redeemed community of people who are made brand new by Jesus' death on the cross. This new organism is His body. It serves Jesus, the head. The physical body serves the mind's desires, and this is also true of the Church. It consists of many members but with the same purpose: Christ. Many parts but with the same mind: Christ. So, what should you do with your life? Whatever Christ says to you. He, though, has said it simply, *abide in me* (John 15:4).

Christ is all and in all. He is first place in all of creation. He does not live to serve you. He lives to give you life, but never be mistaken of the very source of your life: Christ. You are part of His story – it's not the other way around. He is the author and perfecter of your faith – you are not, the pastor is not, the government is not, but He is.

He is bigger than any problem you face. He is bigger than any past struggle you have been engaged with. He is bigger than your present. He is bigger than your future. In fact, your past, present, and future are not even about you; they are about Christ. So maybe we can reword that sentence to say, *He is your past, He is your present, and He is your future.* Think of it this way: before you were even made, He knew what you would do, He knew what you would think, He knew what your quirks would be, He knew what scars would be a part of your body, and He knew what brokenness would hinder you. He knew all this and took it all to the cross with Him so that your past, present, and future could be redeemed and reconciled to Himself so that your story would no longer be yours, but His.

## The Trump Card

The trump card of all creation is Christ. Frank Viola and Leonard Sweet say it best:

All Scripture testifies of Him. The Father exalts Him. The Spirit magnifies Him. The angels worship Him. The early church knew Him as her passion, her message, and the unction of her life. Christ was her specialty. He was her Bridegroom and head. She specialized in nothing else. All told, there's nothing worth pursuing outside of Christ.[2]

Jesus is everything. He is Creator, Redeemer, King, Friend, and Brother. He is more than words can describe, for He is outside of language and time. We cannot express His glory with the capacities of our minds, let alone put it into words that can be understood. Regardless, we try. We try to inch closer to His glory and majesty, knowing that what we come up with is incomplete.

Despite His power, glory, and majesty, we do not worship a Jesus who is far away. He came down to this earth, taking on flesh like you and me, and emptied Himself for all His creation, not wanting anyone to perish, but for all to come to repentance. The giver of life, Jesus, submitted to death for a moment so that He could give you life for eternity.

---

[2] Jesus Manifesto by Frank Viola and Leonard Sweet, Location 592, Kindle.

Death couldn't hold Jesus down. Jesus did exactly what He said He would do and rose on the third day. He came out of that borrowed tomb and spent a little more time amongst the people of 1st Century Israel before returning to His Heavenly glory at the right hand of the throne of the Father.

Jesus not only returned to glory, but He revealed a mystery to us as well. That mystery is Christ in you (Colossians 1:27). Join with me in saying, *mind blown.* Christ has taken up residence in you. You live in Him and He lives in you. A mystery revealed, but a reality so complex and amazing. The Creator of the Universe has looked at you and declared, that'll do.

Wow.

## How Big is Your Jesus?

A trick question? Maybe; for there is only one Jesus. He is who He is - Alpha and Omega, beginning and end, limitless, infinite, eternal, and the embodiment of all Heavenly glory. My prayer is that you would see that Jesus is everything. He is not to be put in a box, for there is no box big enough for Him. He is greater than your little brain can even conjure up. He is greater. He is greater. He is greater.

He is so great that we can all join Frank Viola and Leonard Sweet to declare this:

Christ is all I need. You can strip everything else away from me, and I would still be left with Christ. Take away my gifts and my ministry; take away signs and wonders; take away the sense of His presence; take away my ability to read; and take away every spiritual and religious pursuit I have, and I will still have Christ. And in having Him, I have everything.[3]

## A MIND-BLOWING MYSTERY

Growing up, my dad and I worked in his garage a lot. We worked on various cars, fixing them up, painting them, and tinkering on them. My first official car was a 1977 Chevy Nova. I was stoked when my dad told me that he got it for me. It was certainly a fixer-upper, but I wasn't afraid of working hard to fix it. I was still 14 or so at the time so I had plenty of time before I was ready to drive the car on the streets.

My dad was told that the car had a 383-cubic-inch engine (which is awesome) and a good transmission. The body was in decent condition given the age of the car. The interior of the car was a little rough, but we had time to fix it. No big deal.

---

[3] Jesus Manifesto by Frank Viola and Leonard Sweet, Location 619, Kindle.

It turned out, though, my new car did not have a 383-cubic-inch engine; it had a stock 305-cubic-inch engine and a bad transmission. On top of the bodywork, interior work, and anything else that was bound to turn up, this car was now going to need a new transmission and probably a new engine. In other words, the car was a complete rebuild. Nothing was going to be salvageable. We decided to sell that car. I wish we had kept it as a project car because maybe today it would be all finished up. At least I like to think it would.

But just like how my 1977 Chevy Nova needed a complete rebuild, we also need a complete rebuild. Thankfully, the rebuild is not too big of a job for our God. He is the only one up for the job and He has a very specific way of making that which needs rebuilding better than brand new.

We need everything rebuilt, but the good news is that God has revealed a great mystery to us. This mystery is the key to living as someone who is rebuilt and who is continually being rebuilt.

> The mystery hidden for ages and generations but now revealed to his saints. [27] To them God chose to make known how great among the Gentiles are the riches of the glory of this mystery, which is Christ in you, the hope of glory. – Colossians 1:26-27

A mystery that has been hidden for ages and generations has been revealed to you. It has been revealed to the New Testament Church of which all who follow Christ are a part. This mystery is Christ in you. You have been redeemed, made new, and have also been given a gift: Christ in you.

You and I are not dealing with 305-cubic-inch stock engine with a bad transmission anymore. *Christ in you* means that we are totally rebuilt and supercharged by the Holy Spirit. We have the best of the best parts now, for it is Christ in us. The infinite, magnificent power of God has taken up residence in us. We are not who we used to be; we are something new.

I had a conversation with my wife about how we can never fully know each other and how I often think about what it's like to be her and to be married to me. We were sitting at the dining room table and I asked her if she had ever thought about what it would be like to truly know me. I often wonder what she is thinking and what she is feeling in a given moment. I often wonder what made her decide that marrying me was a good idea. What does she think when I say stupid things – not how does she react, but what does she think deep down? But the reality is, we have a limit to how much we can truly know one another. There's a gap between us that will always be there.

Unlike my relationship with my awesome wife, the Creator of the Universe knows little ole' me inside and out. There is nothing about me that He does not know. And now the mystery has been revealed – Christ in us. Not only has Christ come down from His throne and taken on flesh to die a death for us, but He has also taken up residence in us. He knows us intimately.

The glory and power of Christ has come down and now dwells in us. How profound is that?! We're talking about the God of the Universe deciding that the bodies of the people who make up the Church are good places for Him to take up residence. Instead of choosing a glorious residence, complete with all amenities, God has looked upon you and me and has declared, "That will do."

The power of Christ, the compassion of Christ, Christ Himself, dwells in you. He lives in you, works in you, lives through you, and works through you. You are not left to yourself to live out the Christian life. You are blessed because God has given you the ultimate gift: Himself. He knows you need Him. He knows you will fail without Him. After all, He promised that He would never leave you (Matthew 28:20).

Jesus told His disciples that the Father would send the Holy Spirit *in His name*. "But the Helper, the Holy Spirit, whom the Father will send in my name, he will teach you all things and bring to your remembrance all that I have said to you" (John 14:26). In an attempt to understand the Trinity a little here, let us understand *Christ in you* as the indwelling of the Holy Spirit. God sent the Holy Spirit to live inside of you, to work through you, to work in you, "for it is God who works in you, both to will and to work for his good pleasure" (Philippians 2:13). As simple as it could have been to have the New Testament writers refer to the Holy Spirit in one way, this is not what we see. It's also not what we see in the Old Testament writings either. Instead of always referring to the Holy Spirit as such, He is referenced as the *Spirit of God*, *Spirit of Christ*, *Spirit of the Lord*, *Spirit*, *Holy Spirit*, *Helper*, *Comforter*, *Counselor*, *Advocate*, *the Seal*, and *Spirit of Life* (just to name a few).

In all things, the Holy Spirit points us to the life of Christ. He comforts us, leads us, convicts us, teaches us, seals us, strengthens us, equips us, gifts us, transforms us, intercedes for us, and unites us to the body of Christ. Since the Spirit has come, we can experience the presence of God in us. He brings us from where we were to where God wants us to be. Submitting to the Spirit's leading is the foundation of the way of the crucified.

This truth, this reality, is where much of contemporary Christian writing falls short. This is rarely lifted up as the focus of the Christian life. So many books are devoted to living a certain way, to overcoming struggles, to growing in service, to prioritizing the things of God, and so many more topics. Rarely do I find books, no matter the topic within Christian literature, emphasizing this reality of the indwelling of Christ/Holy Spirit.

This is where everything must start because this *is* where everything starts. The indwelling of Christ is the only reason why we can be transformed and are being transformed into who God wants us to be. This is not something that we can duplicate or substitute for something else. This is vital and elementary to our understanding of how God works in and through us.

We have been crucified to life because of the death, resurrection, and indwelling of Jesus. How often do you hear those three things mentioned in the same sentence?

## GOD'S GRAND PLAN

God's plan from the beginning was not just to save you. As we have seen, His plan was to also live in you and for you to live in Him. This can be seen throughout the New Testament. As one example, Paul speaks to the Christians in first-Century Ephesus about God's grand and marvelous plan. Paul tells them that he has been given the keys to another mystery "which was not made known to the sons of men in other generations as it has now been revealed to his [God's] holy apostles and prophets by the Spirit" (Ephesians 3:5). The Spirit revealed the mystery to

Paul and the holy apostles, and Paul is now sharing that mystery with the Christians in Ephesus.

What is this second mystery? Paul says, "This mystery is that the Gentiles are fellow heirs, members of the same body, and partakers of the promise in Christ Jesus through the gospel" (Ephesians 3:6). The mystery is that the chasm that separated Jew and everyone else is now no more. There is no gap, for Christ has filled the gap with Himself. Because of what Christ has done, all people have the opportunity to be adopted into the family of God and to become joint heirs, parts of the same body, that is Christ, and partakers in the same promise: the salvation of their souls and the indwelling of Christ. You see, the mystery is *Christ in you*, but Paul shows the effect of this reality, which is now available, in this new mystery, to all people no matter their nationality and race. The chosen people are now no longer a single race, but a people who get to go to God in faith through Christ. The community of the crucified is made up of people from every walk of life and from every background. It's a beautiful thing.

In a country that is one full generation removed from the civil rights movement, we find ourselves continuing to struggle through this difference in race. We have acts of hatred still occurring in this *land of the free* where it is written that *all men are created equal*. People are struggling to make sense of the hatred that came to pass in Charleston (Summer 2015) where a young man went into a black congregation and opened fire after spending an hour with them in a Bible study.

As one should expect, we found the unthinkable happen in response to this man's act of vengeance. The people in that church, the family and friends of those who were killed, approached that young man and showed him forgiveness, grace, and love. We should expect the Church to be out in front of issues like race, for the Church is a redeemed people of all nations, all races. The Church is made up of all walks of life, yet it is united. The Church is unified and joined together to the same body, not because of some great list of talking points, but because the Church is the dwelling place of the Holy Spirit who speaks through the Church and points people back to Jesus.

## Boldness and Access

It happens so often and so easily: people put their understanding of their earthly fathers on the Heavenly Father, Jesus Christ, and the Holy Spirit. Dads everywhere are confronted with a multitude of opportunities to give their children a positive or negative outlook on who God is. Too often children approach their dads, hoping to spend time with them, only to find that their dads are too busy. They are too consumed by other things. When they get interrupted by their children, they lash out with something akin to, "I'm busy, get out!" The children learn to be cautious when approaching their dads, and eventually stop approaching, because the outcome is the same. Their dads are too consumed with the game, too busy with a project, or too behind at work to spend time with them.

It's a tragic reality for so many and I hope it is not one that resonates with you. If it does, though, you have a gigantic barrier in front of you that is keeping you from approaching God the way you should. No matter who your dad is, what he is like, or how good or bad he is, you don't have to settle with his image when you look to God. In fact, there is a promise that, in Jesus Christ, "we have boldness and access because of our faith in him" (Ephesians 3:12). You have access to Him and you can go to Him with boldness. Unlike the experiences of many people with their dads, you can go to God with the confidence that only comes from knowing that you are invited to come, that you are going to be heard, and that you will receive His full attention when you do so.

No longer do you need to believe that you are annoying your Heavenly Father when you go to Him. You may have felt that way when going to your earthly father, but that is not the case with your Father. He absolutely

looks forward to every interaction with you. He does not
get consumed with the game, a project, or work. He
always welcomes you into His presence and enjoys
spending time with you.

## Christianity: Missing the Boat

One of my biggest frustrations within the Church today
is that certain passages are picked out from Paul's letters
and emphasized outside of their context. In other words,
I often hear pastors preach on a passage that is all about
*not doing* certain sins, but if you go back to the preceding
context of where they are focusing you'll see the whole
basis for Paul's argument for *right living*. But instead of
going back to examine his whole argument and reasoning
for speaking on moral issues, they preach a message that
could be summed up with *do better, you Christians!*

In Ephesians 3:14-21, Paul shares with the Ephesian
Christians what he prays for on their behalf. This is what
he says:

> [14] For this reason I bow my knees before the
> Father, [15] from whom every family in heaven and on
> earth is named, [16] that according to the riches of his
> glory he may grant you to be strengthened with power
> through his Spirit in your inner being, [17] so that Christ
> may dwell in your hearts through faith—that you,
> being rooted and grounded in love, [18] may have

strength to comprehend with all the saints what is the breadth and length and height and depth, [19] and to know the love of Christ that surpasses knowledge, that you may be filled with all the fullness of God.

[20] Now to him who is able to do far more abundantly than all that we ask or think, according to the power at work within us, [21] to him be glory in the church and in Christ Jesus throughout all generations, forever and ever. Amen.

Paul prays for three specific things on behalf of the Ephesian Christians.

1. He prays that they would be strengthened with power through the Holy Spirit so that Christ may dwell in their hearts as a result of their faith. This is a reiteration of the mystery that is revealed: Christ in you.

2. He prays that they would be rooted and grounded in love, able to comprehend the vastness of the love of Christ.

3. He prays that they would be filled with all the fullness of God. Again, we see his desire that the reality of the mind-blowing mystery would be revealed in their lives.

Notice what Paul does not pray for. He does not pray that they would be perfect Christians who never sin and who are always nice. His prayer is for the deeper things that end up causing Christians to live the abundant life – the life that is characterized by Christ. Without laying the groundwork for right living, we often completely miss the boat for our basis in right living.

Colossians 3:1-5 shows us something similar to Ephesians. Before Paul begins to tell the Christians in Colossae how to live, he reminds them of the foundation on which they live and exist. He reminds them of their new reality – their new identity. This is what he says:

> If then you have been raised with Christ, seek the things that are above, where Christ is, seated at the right hand of God. Set your minds on things that are above, not on things that are on earth. For you have died, and your life is hidden with Christ in God. When Christ who is your life appears, then you also will appear with him in glory.

> Put to death therefore what is earthly in you: sexual immorality, impurity, passion, evil desire, and covetousness, which is idolatry.

Since you have been crucified to life (raised with Christ), your mind and focus need to be on the things that are of Heaven and not of this earth. You have died to that old way of living, that old way that is characterized by following your passions and desires. That you is gone, for you now live as the crucified you. Your life is Christ, nothing more, nothing less.

Therefore, put to death that which is already dead in you: your sins that defined the old you. You have been completely made into someone new – brand new. The new you does not live like the old you. Naturally, then, those dead things are to leave you.

## A FOUNDATION FOR RIGHT LIVING

As we have seen this foundation for right living fully play out in Colossians 3, we'll now see the continuation of Paul's argument in his letter to the Ephesians. After Paul tells the Ephesian Christians what he had been praying for on their behalf, he shifts to urging them to walk in a worthy manner. This is what he says:

> I therefore, a prisoner for the Lord, urge you to walk in a manner worthy of the calling to which you have been called, with all humility and gentleness, with patience, bearing with one another in love, eager to maintain the unity of the Spirit in the bond of peace.
> – Ephesians 4:1-3

My 1977 Nova with a stock 305-cubic-inch engine and a bad transmission couldn't drive like I wanted it to. I wanted it to have the 450+ horsepower expected with the 383-cubic-inch-stroker engine I thought it had, but it only had a measly 110 horsepower. It was what it was – a stock Nova with a bad transmission in need of a ton of work.

We are all like my 1977 Nova before Christ – in need of a ton of work. When we begin to put morality as our goal rather than Christ, we are expecting our 305-cubic-inch engine to magically become that 383 stroker. It doesn't work. What must happen is for Christ to be our goal in all things, and when that is the case, the Holy Spirit rebuilds us into what He wants us to be: brand new with a brand new engine and transmission. But here's the thing: it doesn't all happen at once. It takes time, just like a car rebuild takes time. You can't expect to be completely rebuilt the day after you become a Christ-follower. God continues to work on you for the rest of your life, always fine-tuning, always tweaking.

Even though it takes time, it is happening, nonetheless. We are being made into something brand new and because of this, we should live in our new reality. It is our calling and Paul is urging us to live in light of that. What does that look like? It looks like humility, gentleness, patience, and love. It looks like the fruit of the Spirit. It looks like a community of people, the Church, living in light of their new reality – Christ in them – and being a unified organism.

As the Holy Spirit has His way with us, we will "no longer be children, tossed to and fro by the waves and carried about by every wind of doctrine, by human cunning, by craftiness in deceitful schemes" (Ephesians 4:14). If our foundation for right living is our own power and strength, we will surely be tossed about by every temptation, failing to even fight. However, with the Holy Spirit living in us, guiding us, and spurring us on to good works, we will be strengthened to fight temptation and to live in light of our calling in Christ Jesus.

It all starts with Christ crucified and it all ends with Christ in you, giving you abundant life. Without emphasizing the reality of the crucifixion to life, you are but a mere will-powered human being trying to do something you cannot do: live right. The only basis for living a holy life is Christ in you. That is it.

When this begins to happen, the following will take place:

> [15] Rather, speaking the truth in love, we are to grow up in every way into him who is the head, into Christ, [16] from whom the whole body, joined and held together by every joint with which it is equipped, when each part is working properly, makes the body grow so that it builds itself up in love. – Ephesians 4:15-16

As the Spirit conforms the Church into the shape of the Son, the truth will be spoken in love, people will grow up in Christ, and every part will work properly, causing the body – the Church – to grow up and be built in love. This is the natural result of a group of people who have been crucified to life by Christ. Unity is no abstract idea or result of wishful thinking; it is the body of Christ held together by Christ Himself. What unites the Church? Christ in the Church! Unity does not come to the Church by great leaders, great pastors, or great preaching. It comes from our great Savior. It comes from God residing in us. He unites people from all backgrounds, all upbringings, all races, and all languages. The Church will be more unified when she remembers her reality: she has been crucified to life by Christ.

# SECTION TWO: THE WAY OF THE CRUCIFIED

## Chapter 5

# Up for Whatever

---

*Then he said to his disciples, "The harvest is plentiful,*
*but the laborers are few; therefore pray earnestly to the*
*Lord of the harvest to send out laborers into his harvest.*
*– Matthew 9:37-38*

In his 2008 movie, *Yes Man*, Jim Carrey plays Carl, a bank loan officer who had become extremely cynical about life. He was negative about everything – that is, until he ran into an old friend who prodded him into tagging along to a motivational seminar. The seminar was entitled, *Yes!* As they arrived to the seminar, Carl quickly realized that that place was the last place he wanted to be. Amid everyone shouting "yes," the speaker zeroed in on the one person in the building who was resisting the shout: Carl. Carl ended up saying a halfhearted "yes," and this began his journey of only being able to say "yes" to people whenever they asked him to do something. Literally to every request, he said "yes." And through that willingness, he saw his life change in more ways than one.

Our culture is full of cynicism. But, unfortunately, our secular culture is not the only place cynicism has decided to infiltrate. Go to any church in our time and you'll encounter stuffy cynics who choke the mission of God. They say "no" when God calls. They say "no" when God propels the vision of His church forward. They say "no" when a leader wants to implement much-needed change.

But here we may be getting ahead of ourselves. The cynicism that is so easily seen in others, first manifests itself in each one of us. It begins like a subtle whisper of doubt and turns into an all-out justification of the word "no." The question is, *what are we saying no to?* No, the better question is, *to whom are we saying no?*

It is at the foundation of those who have tasted God's grace, who have died to self, who have been raised to life, and who have been indwelled by the living Christ, to become a *yes man,* or a *yes woman,* toward God. When God tells us what to do, our response ought to be "yes, Lord." When God tells us where to go, our response ought to be "yes, Lord."

Every fiber in our being is filled with the living Christ, which means every fiber in our being is oriented toward His direction. We don't need a motivational seminar; we have the Creator of the Universe calling us. We can pick up the phone or let it go to voicemail. We're not coerced into automatically say "yes" like Carl was. We have choice in this world. Yet, the way of the crucified begins with this response to God's request: "yes."

## 3 PROPHETS, 3 CALLS, 3 ANSWERS

From the outset of time, we see that God decided to work out His purposes in this world by using people who answered His call on their lives. Three men who experienced and answered the call of God can serve as examples for us. Each of them became a prophet because God called him to be so. Two of them had similar responses, one had a different response, but in the end, each of them followed God on a journey into the unknown. And make no mistake, the unknown is where we are called to as well, because we were not simply saved from damnation but were saved to take part in God's mission.

### Isaiah

The call of Isaiah is one of the most profound passages in Scripture. If you want to read the entire thing, you can find it in Isaiah 6. But for a moment, just imagine having a vision of the throne room of God. Angels are there – not little baby angels dressed in white with cute smiles, but real angels. Imagine the sight: Seraphim with six wings, two to shield their eyes, two to cover their feet, and two to fly, together singing a song to God, "holy, holy, holy." You can't even count them; in fact, you're afraid to even look at them. And then, simultaneously, you hear a voice and you feel the ground shake beneath your feet. Your chest is pounded by the sheer volume of the voice, even more than it would be by standing in the front row of a Metallica concert. If that weren't enough, accompanying the voice and the shaking is smoke filling up the room. All your senses are engaged. You look up. You fall to your face.

Sound intimidating? Sound awe-inspiring? You are standing in the place of Isaiah in the throne room of the Most High. For Isaiah, though, *intimidating* doesn't cut it. He was petrified. "Woe is me! For I am lost; for I am a man of unclean lips, and I dwell in the midst of a people of unclean lips; for my eyes have seen the King, the Lord of hosts!" (Isaiah 6:5). In the presence of God, Isaiah felt ruined. He knew his sin because he knew the true God.

But then something happened in response to Isaiah's declaration: one of the Seraphim flew to Isaiah with a burning coal. Standing before Isaiah, the Seraphim took the burning coal and touched it to Isaiah's mouth and declared, "this has touched your lips; your guilt is taken away, and your sin atoned for" (Isaiah 6:7). Isaiah had been given new life. And then, as if this was part of the plan all along, the Almighty speaks again saying, "Whom shall I send, and who will go for us?" (Isaiah 6:8a). Isaiah, in that moment, had a choice to make. Would he answer with a "yes" or would he take his forgiveness and say, "thanks God, but I have all I need and want"?

Isaiah's response was perfect: "Here I am! Send me" (Isaiah 6:8b). And with that, Isaiah the prophet was born. In a single moment, Isaiah went from petrified sinner to prophetic servant. He was given a new story, a new beginning, and so it is with us. But Isaiah didn't take that new identity and go about life as usual; he realized that God's call was the natural *next thing* in his life. And so it is with us.

When we come to Christ and surrender to Him, we can rest assured that He will not only save us, transform us, and indwell us, but He will also call us. A life with Christ is truly a life of adventure, because at any moment, He could call us to a certain place to minister to a certain person. And yet, sometimes, He may allow us to go where we decide, loving sacrificially as we embark on the journey.

We must not settle for a mundane life. Instead, we should expect to live abundantly with Christ. And this should raise our level of awareness of the world around us. It should raise our level of expectancy that we do in fact have a part to play in this world we live in.

What we see with Isaiah is that his sins were wiped away, and yet this was not an end in itself. Instead, we see that his sins that were wiped away were the prerequisite for him stepping into God's ultimate plan for his life. And for us, the same is true. We are not saved to simply be saved, but to enter into the abundant life God has before us. And that abundant life begins with Isaiah's declaration, *here I am. Send me.*

## Jeremiah

Unlike Isaiah, Jeremiah wasn't so willing to answer the call of God. He had some apprehension like we do at times. He was a logical thinker who didn't see himself as the *right guy* for the job. But God did, and in the end, that's all that mattered.

All we're told at the beginning of this biblical account is that Jeremiah had the word of the Lord come to him. We don't know what the occasion was. We don't know if he was walking along a road, pondering life in the darkness of night, or going about his work in the midst of the day. Since there isn't much attention given to the occasion, it's likely that it was just a normal day. He was probably going about his routine – same stuff, different day. And many times, when God speaks, it's when we least expect Him to.

What does God say to Jeremiah? He says the phrase you may have heard preached or have seen on a poster: "Before I formed you in the womb I knew you, and before you were born I consecrated you; I appointed you a prophet to the nations" (Jeremiah 1:5). What would you say to that? What argument *could* you make, let alone *would* you make? *I created you, I knew you even before that, and I have given you your mission in life – prophet to the nations.* That seems like an air-tight statement. But Jeremiah attempts a rebuttal, still.

Jeremiah responds with, "Ah, Lord God! Behold, I do not know how to speak, for I am only a youth" (Jeremiah 1:6). It's like Jeremiah is saying, *I know you created me and all that, but you've forgotten two things: I'm a terrible speaker and I'm really young.* Jeremiah is like us. He does a great job at reminding himself why he can't do something. He sees God's call, but even more, he sees his shortcomings. Here he is, having a conversation with God, and he still sees more of his weakness than he sees God's power. But again, we shouldn't be too hard on Jeremiah. We do the same thing.

God's response is better than a golden ticket for Willy Wonka's Chocolate Factory: "Do not say, 'I am only a youth'; for to all to whom I send you, you shall go, and whatever I command you, you shall speak" (Jeremiah 1:7). God seems to be saying that Jeremiah needs to be up for whatever God tells him. Jeremiah's rebuttals were nothing in the face of the One who created him. God already knew Jeremiah's shortcomings and He already knows ours as well. He wasn't surprised that Jeremiah responded this way either.

Getting to the heart of the age issue, God assures Jeremiah, "Do not be afraid of them, for I am with you to deliver you, declares the Lord" (Jeremiah 1:8). And getting to the heart of the speech issue, God declares, "Behold, I have put my words in your mouth" (Jeremiah 1:9b). God is so good like that. Even though, from His perspective, our fears and weaknesses are as small as a grain of sand, He still addresses them. He doesn't just tell Jeremiah that his age and speech are pointless rebuttals, but He speaks to Jeremiah's heart and reassures him of His power, His presence, and His confidence in His calling to be a prophet.

Imagine how Jeremiah must have been feeling in that moment. The Creator of the Cosmos spoke to him, called him to an assignment that he was designed to do, and compassionately and firmly addressed his concerns with promises. Surely, he had a deep sense of awe and security, anticipation and calm, excitement and faith. In the same way, we can expect God to deal with us gently as well. He will listen to our rebuttals, He will take into account our fears, and He will respond with His promises which can be trusted for all time and beyond.

And with that, Jeremiah began his new journey. He got to work living into his new-found reality. He answered the call and spoke the very words of God. When God calls us, which He certainly will (and likely already has), and we respond with rebuttal after rebuttal, will we listen to His promises and act accordingly? It is in our very design to live out the calling God has for us. We are to be a part of His mission and to allow Him to lead us wherever He desires for us to go.

## Ezekiel

At first glance, it appears Ezekiel's call has much less flare, much less intrigue, and much less pizazz than the calls of Isaiah and Jeremiah. But make no mistake, this encounter is filled with something truly beautiful – truly awe-inspiring.

*Get up, we need to talk.* And so, Ezekiel's call begins like this. From Ezekiel's perspective, something powerful happened as God was speaking to him. He wasn't overwhelmed to the point of falling to his face like Isaiah and he wasn't ready to argue like Jeremiah. Instead, Ezekiel was given assurance before he had a moment to doubt what God was saying to him. From his perspective, this is what happened: "And as he spoke to me, the Spirit entered into me and set me on my feet, and I heard him speaking to me" (Ezekiel 2:2). That's an interesting way of putting it. He heard God speaking from the beginning, but when God's Spirit entered, he stood and it seemed as though he could hear more clearly.

Ezekiel's call is unique because God does all the talking. Ezekiel doesn't get a word in, but that doesn't seem to alarm him because what God says is enough for him. God tells him that he is going to speak against a land of rebels who are stubborn and hard-headed – not exactly the most inspiring of jobs. But God follows Ezekiel's job description by urging him to not be afraid. The interesting thing, though, is that God doesn't give Ezekiel a reason for not being afraid. He simply charges him to not fear their words, their looks, or their actions. But on what basis was Ezekiel to not be afraid? It's not like God told Ezekiel that He would always protect him. Maybe it was implied. Or maybe something deeper is going on.

Ezekiel, from the beginning of his encounter with the Almighty God, seemed to be calm enough to stay quiet and listen. I believe this is because God, from the outset, knew what Ezekiel needed most: His presence. God's Spirit entered Ezekiel in the beginning of God's monologue and Ezekiel seemed to be profoundly affected by this. Because of God's Spirit entering him, Ezekiel felt a close connection with God, His words, and the calling set before him. In a way, God doing this for Ezekiel in the midst of calling him to be a prophet is a shadow of what God does for us through Jesus. As Paul reveals in 2 Corinthians, God has "given us his Spirit in our hearts as a guarantee" (1:22b). And what is that guarantee? The guarantee of what is to ultimately come is the return of Christ. But for Ezekiel, God seemed to show him that he could be assured that he was called to be a prophet and that God was going to be with him every step of the way.

It's easy for us to read what happened with Ezekiel and think *I wish that could happen to me and that I could experience God's presence like that.* But for those of us who have been crucified with Christ, we live with God's presence in an even better way than Ezekiel did.

## CONNECT THE DOTS

Many times, reading Scripture is like a version of connect the dots. You remember doing this when you were younger, right? Each dot is numbered and you simply draw a line from one dot to the next and go on until every dot is chronologically connected. As we look at the way God called each of these three prophets from the Old Testament, a picture of connect the dots is taking shape and we need to connect the dots.

### Isaiah's Sin

Let's begin by going back to Isaiah. He had a vision where he was in the throne room of God, and it was there that he fell to his face because of the utter holiness of God coming face-to-face with his sinfulness. He saw himself as a completely ruined individual and knew that he was unworthy to be in the presence of the Almighty God. But what does God do in response? He sent a Seraphim to Isaiah who put a burning coal to his mouth. And while this was happening, God declared that his guilt was taken away and that his sin was atoned for. Surely, we wonder how this was possible, for Isaiah lived hundreds of years before Jesus came onto the scene.

So, on what basis is Isaiah's sin atoned for and guilt wiped away? It is credited to none other than Jesus Christ. Speaking of Christ, Paul says this in Romans 3:25-26:

> whom God put forward as a propitiation by his blood, to be received by faith. This was to show God's righteousness, because in his divine forbearance he had passed over former sins. [26] It was to show his righteousness at the present time, so that he might be just and the justifier of the one who has faith in Jesus.

Do you see the last statement in verse 25? God, in His ability to see the entire story, was able to atone for the all the sin of Isaiah through the sacrifice of His Son, Jesus. So, the sins that are nailed to the cross are not just the sins of the people at the time of and after the cross, but they are the sins of the people *before* the cross as well. Isaiah, the prophet who spoke of the suffering Servant hundreds of years before He arrived in a manger, was saved because of what that Servant – Jesus – suffered.

Therefore, the thing that Isaiah experienced that opened the door for him to live into his calling is the same thing we experience that opens the door to us living abundant life. Isaiah's sins were paid for so that he could go on and live into the destiny God had for him. We must also begin here. We will never be able to live into God's plan for our lives if we are still bound by our sin. But thank God that in His divine wisdom, Jesus did what He did.

It's easy for us to think that God only calls those who are like Isaiah – seemingly special. But the reality is, Isaiah wasn't very special. What made him unique was that God wiped away his sin. What made his story one that we know today was his willingness to be up for whatever. If you are in Christ, your sin has been wiped away as well. And what will make your story one worth telling is your willingness to be up for whatever God has for you to do.

## Jeremiah's Identity

What led to Isaiah being called by God is similar to what leads us to being called by God. The same is true for Jeremiah. If you refer back to how God called Jeremiah, you'll see that God spoke directly to the depths of Jeremiah's identity. He explained that He knew Jeremiah more than Jeremiah knew himself. "Before I formed you in the womb I knew you," and to that we can simply say, wow!

The picture is becoming clearer. The dots are connecting and what is becoming of them is absolutely beautiful. The echo of what God said to Jeremiah is directed at us in the New Testament: "For we are his workmanship, created in Christ Jesus for good works, which God prepared beforehand, that we should walk in them" (Ephesians 2:10). Surely what God says to Jeremiah can be said to us as well. Before God decided to create us, He knew us. But while God appointed Jeremiah to be a prophet, God has prepared all kinds of good works before us – works for us to walk in.

As God's words to Jeremiah surely took the pressure off him, His words to us should do the same. What I've found is that when we begin talking about the *calling of God*, we struggle with the idea that God has or would call us all to something. But the thing is, He may not be calling you to become an overseas missionary (maybe He is?), but He *is* calling you to walk into what He has set before you.

But like Jeremiah, many of us, even to the statement above, want to give God fifteen reasons why we're not equipped to do what He has called us to do. Jeremiah started with two reasons: his speaking ability and his age.

In his mind, to be a prophet, he needed to be a wise sage who could speak with power. But God wasn't interested in calling the person Jeremiah had in his mind to this specific appointment. He had Jeremiah in mind from the beginning and He wanted Jeremiah to be himself and to walk into the calling He had set before him.

We must realize this same truth in our lives as well. God is not calling us to be someone else; He is calling us to let Him use us. We don't need to be the wisest Bible scholar, or the most eloquent of speakers, or even the most compassionate of servants. We must simply be our crucified selves and believe that God is powerful enough to use us despite our shortcomings.

God has set before you specific good things to do. Whether you walk in them is up to you. Whether you're equipped or not is of no question. God, your Creator, knows you so deeply that He has prepared you to do exactly what He has designed you to do. Be up for whatever. Let Him use you.

## Ezekiel's Assurance and God's Presence

There are only a couple of dots left to connect before we see the completeness of this picture. When Ezekiel was called, the Spirit of God entered him and he was continually reminded to not be afraid. Ezekiel's call was to go to a place filled with people rebelling against God. So, the implication was that as God's prophet, he would also be rebelled against. And as for us and the time we live, this shouldn't sound unfamiliar.

In the midst of a culture that is running from God and the way of His kingdom, we need God's assurance. We need His presence. We need God to whisper to us and speak to us what He spoke to Ezekiel. And yet He has. Through Jesus Christ, we get a promise, a guarantee that we will always be accompanied through life by God. Jesus said this Himself, "behold, I am with you always, to the end of the age" (Matthew 28:20b). And we know this theologically; we know this is the truth. The question quickly becomes this: will we believe it to the point that it alters the way we live?

We've already discovered that the reality of the crucified is that Christ is in us today – that His work wasn't done with His rising to heaven, but that it continues today, in and through us. Ezekiel experienced a glimpse of what we experience every day now. God's assurance to him was enough for him to take a step of faith toward a land of unknown – toward a future of unknown. For Ezekiel, realizing that God would be with him every step of the way had to have given him a confidence that couldn't be shaken. His fear was extinguished by the presence of the Almighty.

Our problem isn't a lack of knowing, but a lack of trusting that what we know is actually true. We can be reminded day by day of the works of God. We can read what He has spoken to us through His word: the Bible. We can know what God has done, but we run into trouble when God calls us to live as though what we have learned and what He has said are true.

## From Dots to Completed Picture

We've taken a deep dive into the callings of Isaiah, Jeremiah, and Ezekiel, three prophets of God who had been called to walk into what God had prepared for them. From God's interactions with them, we could simply understand that the way of the crucified begins with being up for whatever. But if we ended there, we'd miss the broader picture God has drawn.

Friend, don't ever doubt that God has something in mind for your life. Everything God did for these prophets, He has done for you.

Isaiah's sins were wiped away so that he could walk into God's calling for his life. If you are in Christ, the same can be said for you. What used to be a barrier between you and God has now been destroyed by the blood of the Perfect Lamb.

Jeremiah's doubts about himself were confronted with the reality that God had known him before he was even in existence. He was shown that he was made for this. You can rest in the reality that God knows you just as intimately. You can take to the bank the reality that God has designed you to walk in the good things He has prepared for you to do.

Ezekiel's fears were laid to rest when God's Spirit entered his body, giving him assurance that he would never be alone. If Christ is the Lord of your life, you also enjoy the presence of God's Spirit in your life every single day. You will never experience another second on this earth as someone who is alone. Christ in you is your new reality.

The broader picture, then, is that God's work in the lives of these prophets of yesterday is His present work in the lives of the crucified of today. His story isn't finished and His work isn't done. He has a mission to see fulfilled, and He is choosing to do so through you. Today.

## GIFTED AND CALLED

God is creative in a way that cannot be described. Every single person on this earth is different from the next. Some may look alike, some may think alike, some may act alike, but overall we are all different. And while we live in a world that has a hard time with differences, it is the people's differences inside the Church that make the Church a unique force for God's mission to be realized.

Here's a truth that is vital for you to walk away with and let seep deep into your heart: you are uniquely gifted by God to live out what He has and will call you to. God has done a work in your heart through Christ, and He desires to do a work through you by His Spirit. And this is the case for all of us, for "to each is given the manifestation of the Spirit for the common good" (1 Corinthians 12:7). Throughout the rest of 1 Corinthians 12, Paul describes some examples of gifts given to people by the Spirit of God. We won't go into depth right now on all the different gifts, but if you'd like to learn more about how God has gifted you, go to **BrandonKelley.org/gifted**.

In addition to giving examples of the gifts of the Spirit, Paul goes on to explain the nature of the Church by giving us a picture of how it works. The picture he gives is the anatomy of a human body. Now, let me just say, don't have a panic attack. You won't be required to go back to your time in High School when you had to memorize the bones of the human body. You may even remember a song that you sang to help you memorize them all. But again, no advanced knowledge required. Paul keeps this elementary. Thank you, Paul.

God's people make up the many parts of one body. This is the basic picture Paul gives. Each one of us, even in our local church body (now you see why it's referred to as a church "body" – go tell your friends, they'll be impressed) makes up the entire body of Christ. Now, we won't begin to try and deduce who is what body part – I don't think that's Paul's point. Instead, Paul shows us the way we ought to view the Church (the people) as an intimately connected body: "If one member suffers, all suffer together; if one member is honored, all rejoice together" (1 Corinthians 12:26). If you've ever dealt with emotional pain or physical pain, you know this to be true. Also, if you've ever been over-the-moon excited about something, you know this is to be true.

## No Lone Ranger Body Parts

Imagine the sight: a disembodied foot running in all directions, trying to *do the work of the Lord*. The foot has no calf muscles, no ankle, no toes, no thigh to lift it off the ground, let alone eyes to see where to go. Can you see it? It may be easier for you to see a disembodied hand running around. That is, if you are familiar with the Addams Family movies from the 90's. Can you see it? It's not a pretty sight. It's rather frightening. And to think, this is exactly what it's like when Christ followers decide to go about life as a lone ranger.

You know who they are – you may even be one of them. They are the "can't fit inside a box" type of people who are always doing something for the Lord, but they don't belong to a local church. This is not how God designed things to be. Certainly, God wants them to exercise their entrepreneurial personality, but He desires for them to do so in the context of the connected body of Christ: the Church.

They aren't only those who are entrepreneurially bent, but they are also the people who say they love Jesus but don't love the church. They have their reasons why they left a local church, but instead of finding a home within another local church, they have given up on being in this unique community altogether. You know who they are – you may even be one of them.

God has, from the start of the Church, had local groups of people gather with one another, do life with one another, and live out His mission together. If your arm was cut off from the rest of your body, that arm would quickly die and you would be left suffering. God's Church suffers when His people refuse to be a part of a local church. How can we suffer together if we're not with others? How can we rejoice together if we're not with others? It simply doesn't work.

We all need each other. We may not be prophets, but we do need people who will speak truth in our lives. We may not be helpers, but we do need those who are willing to help us in our lives. We may not be administrators, but we do need those who are leaders and organizers in our lives. But here's the thing: this isn't about us. It's about God's people working together to reach a dying world. The crucified don't live apart from the world; they go into the world, using their gifts, and letting God work through them to reach those who are far from Him. And the only way this is going to be done is through God's Church being a unified body.

## The Gift and Calling to Start From

"And I will show you a still more excellent way" (1 Corinthians 12:31b). The answer you get is dependent upon the question you ask. It's clear that if you read 1 Corinthians, the people who Paul is writing to are concerned with several minor issues, but they all stem from a larger issue that Paul is seeking to address. In chapter 12 of 1 Corinthians, Paul answers their request to know more about spiritual gifts. It's not that spiritual gifts are unimportant so Paul goes ahead and addresses the topic for them. But then at the end, he pivots to the real conversation they should be having. Like a doctor who diagnoses the symptoms and identifies the underlying problem, Paul goes to work.

If you've spent any time in church, you may be familiar with part of 1 Corinthians 13. Surely, if you've been to a wedding recently, you heard it read. It's known as the love chapter. But please, please suspend your prior knowledge of this chapter so we can see it in its full context.

After just getting done addressing the topic of spiritual gifts and how the Church is made up of many parts, Paul dives into the gift and calling we all must start from. This is how he puts it:

> If I speak in the tongues of men and of angels, but have not love, I am a noisy gong or a clanging cymbal. And if I have prophetic powers, and understand all mysteries and all knowledge, and if I have all faith, so as to remove mountains, but have not love, I am nothing. If I give away all I have, and if I deliver up my body to be burned, but have not love, I gain nothing. – 1 Corinthians 13:1-3

As people who have been crucified with Christ, who have been raised to life, who have been given a brand-new identity, and who have been indwelled by His Spirit, we are to, in everything, love God and love people. If we are from God and for God, love is our most foundational gifting and our most foundational calling.

We could speak God's word with power, but would be worthless if we don't love. We could be faith-filled risk takers, but would be worthless if we don't love. Love is the way of the crucified. It's our heartbeat. It's our greatest gift and our greatest calling. If we fail at loving

God and loving others, we fail at everything, for love is everything for those who follow Jesus.

## Keep the Main Thing in its Proper Place

We should all take time to discover how God has uniquely gifted us and called us, but we should never forget that we are all, first and foremost, gifted to and called to love God and love others. The way of the crucified begins here and ends here. As we move forward, love must be our constant. It must be the filter through which we see, hear, and move in this world. If we can get this right, everything else will fall into place.

CHAPTER 6

# ANOMALIES FOR GOD'S GLORY

---

*We must allow the Word of God to confront us, to
disturb our security, to undermine our complacency and to
overthrow our patterns of thought and behavior. – John
Stott*

Excitement and anticipation filled our hearts. To pull it
off I had to park a few blocks away along with about
thirty other people. It was my buddy's birthday party – a
surprise party. The sun was out, the air was warm, and the
sky was clear. Thankfully this was the case since we were
all outside in the backyard, out of sight from the front of
the house. The timing had to be perfect. The
coordination with others had to be superb. It takes
thought to pull off a surprise of any kind, let alone a
surprise party.

After a few false alarms, he arrived. Prompted to go to the backyard by a friend who was serving as his host, he turned the corner. The view of his home gave way to the view of his backyard with one synchronized shout of *Surprise!*, which ignited a response of just that: surprise.

Surprises are powerful. They can be used to make someone feel extra special, but they can be used in other ways, too. Just recently, the church I serve at (The Crossing) purchased a campus complete with three buildings and 54 acres. For the first time in over five years, our staff is in an office environment together. When we made the move into the offices, my family and I were on vacation so I got to move into my office after everyone else was a week into the new setup. I arranged my time off so that I would return to the office and get back to work on a Saturday. My plan was to use the day to get settled into my new office. After I had been there for a little while I noticed some kind of sound coming from another room in the building. I figured one of my coworkers was in the building. So, I went to say hi.

Walking down the hall and into the break room, I opened the already cracked door. Our lead pastor, Kenny White, was on the other side of that cracked door. And as soon as he noticed that he was no longer alone in our office building he tried to kick at the door to escape my ninja attack. As he was kicking, I proceeded to tell him who I was and began to laugh at what had just happened. Once he realized that I was not an assassin hired by a church member, he laughed and greeted me. Surprises can sometimes be great – they can even make your lead pastor tremble in fear. But there are still other kinds of surprises. One kind we're going to dive into is a surprise Jesus used in His teaching to His followers.

## SURPRISING STATEMENTS OF JESUS

Picture yourself as one of Jesus' disciples where Jesus choses a beautiful setting to do some teaching. You'll remember the moment not just because of the amazing scenery, but also because of what Jesus says. It will have been the greatest teaching you had ever heard. And from the outset, He has your attention. He has your attention, not because of some elaborate story He tells, but because every statement He makes is one that makes you scratch your head. You are beyond surprised at the counter-intuitive things He says.

### Heirs of a Kingdom

It's not who you expected. Jesus said, "Blessed are the poor in spirit, for theirs is the kingdom of heaven" (Matthew 5:3). He wastes no time and begins challenging your understanding of economics and success.

When we think of heirs to a kingdom, we think of princes, princesses, and their children. We think of royalty, of success, of money, of status, of riches. And this is why Jesus' statement is so surprising. It challenges everything you and I think about success, especially if you're an American like me.

We live in a world where weakness is something to be taken advantage of, not blessed. We know that we shouldn't show our emotions too much, especially if they are of sadness, because we are all too familiar with being exploited by those who want to get ahead. Instead, we are to have confidence and to *keep our heads up*. But it's interesting: Jesus says the ones who are blessed by God, and heirs to the kingdom of heaven, are those who are poor in spirit.

Certainly, we want to be fellow heirs to that kingdom. And surely, as we have seen thus far, we are. As those who have been crucified to life, our inheritance is the kingdom of heaven. But you may be wondering, what does Jesus mean? What does it really look like to be poor in spirit? Well, He answers this question with the next eight surprising statements.

## Eight Surprising Characteristics of Heirs to the Kingdom of Heaven

It was with that one statement that your attention shifts from the beautiful views of your classroom to the Rabbi you have been following. Jesus has your attention in His hands because He knows you want to be a part of this kingdom He speaks of. He knows that you've been having a hard time being under Roman rule. He knows that your greatest desire is to see Israel rise in power once again and reach its full potential as God's chosen nation. But He also knows that what He has in store for you is much better than what you desire. And so, He continues.

*"Blessed are those who mourn, for they shall be comforted" (Matthew 5:4).* I don't know about you, but it's hard for me to mourn. I don't get emotional that often, even in times where lots of people are very emotional. And I think I know why: I have experienced significant pain in my past, but instead of fully mourning, I disconnected myself from the world as much as I could. And in doing so, I wasn't comforted like I could have been. I was too proud to let people see what I thought were weaknesses in me: sadness and hurt. But I was only hurting myself and robbing others of the blessing it is to comfort someone else.

From first look, Jesus' statement seems to be quite unsurprising, but when we consider how things are in our world, it's easy to see why this actually is surprising. In a world full of brokenness and pain, we do a bad job at providing true comfort to people who are mourning – even if they don't hide it. Our tendency is to give people a designated amount of time to mourn (a time that we come up with on our own) and then expect them to return to normal. That is what we do here in the kingdom of this world. But Jesus gives us a picture of what an heir to the kingdom of heaven looks like by giving us a glimpse at what the kingdom of heaven is like.

Those who are heirs to the kingdom of heaven are ones who presently mourn – not always, but when they have a reason to – and the promise they have is that when they inherit the kingdom of heaven, they will be comforted. Jesus is not simply saying that those who openly mourn will be comforted in this world. To experience true comfort, mourners shall look to a new kingdom. And so, those who mourn now are blessed because of what is in store for them.

*"Blessed are the meek, for they shall inherit the earth" (Matthew 5:5).* If Jesus' last statement seemed to be unsurprising at first, this statement is surely the opposite. We don't see meek people as ones who are inheriting this earth. They are not ones who are in power or ones who are in control. Those who are meek seem to experience exactly the opposite of inheriting the earth; they live simply, they are humble, and they are submissive. These don't seem like characteristics of heirs to this earth. But what if Jesus isn't talking about this earth?

In Revelation 21:1, the apostle John tells what he saw in his revelation from God: "Then I saw a new heaven and a new earth, for the first heaven and the first earth had passed away, and the sea was no more." Here, John is speaking of what will happen in the future, and this goes right along with Jesus' promise of inheritance. He doesn't say the meek *are* inheriting the earth – as if it's a present thing they are experiencing today – but He says they *shall* inherit the earth – as in they surely will.

So then, those who are to inherit the kingdom of heaven are foundationally meek. They are humble, submissive, and ones who live simply. And their promise is that they will inherit the earth – the new earth – which will be our place in the kingdom of heaven. While those who are meek here and now may seem to be taken advantage of and fail to *get ahead* in life, make no mistake, theirs is the kingdom of heaven.

*"Blessed are those who hunger and thirst for righteousness, for they shall be satisfied" (Matthew 5:6).* We don't know that this is the case at all, but maybe the disciples were hungry. Maybe they hadn't had anything to eat or drink for a little while. Thus, here you are, wanting to stop at a drive-thru – even though they didn't exist then – and get some grub, and Jesus does something cruel. You expect Him to say "blessed are those who hunger and thirst for the right kinds of food," but He doesn't say that. He isn't so much concerned with Jewish dietary restrictions in this statement; He is concerned with the desires of your heart.

Every person on this earth has desires. At the depths of our hearts, our desires are the greatest, but what those desires are says a lot about who is Lord of our lives. But it's interesting that Jesus says that those who are desirous of righteousness will be satisfied, because when we look at the world around us, we can clearly see that those who crave after anything *but* righteousness seem to be having those desires satisfied. The last thing on this earth that seems to be satisfied is a desire for righteousness. Instead of encountering more and more of God's good and perfect law being lived out in people, let alone ourselves, we see wickedness rise like the tide of the sea.

This desire for righteousness is one that we can get bites and sips of, but until Christ returns, we won't be satisfied. God's Spirit is presently taking us on a journey toward righteousness, but we won't fully live into that righteousness until we are in the place of our inheritance – the new earth, the kingdom of heaven. But we need not sit and wait; we ought to purposefully pursue that noble desire, for that is what those who have been crucified to life do.

*"Blessed are the merciful, for they shall receive mercy" (Matthew 5:7).* Here you are, sitting and listening to Jesus teach you what your life should look like – if you want to be blessed, of course. And what continues coming to your mind is the example of the religious leaders of your day,

especially after Jesus says this statement. Growing up, you would have seen these "men of God" keep away from the lowly and the hurting in fear of becoming unclean. In your mind, this is what you were supposed to do. And even after following this Rabbi, Jesus of Nazareth, you defaulted to the ways you had been taught prior to following Jesus. But now, you're beginning to realize that Jesus is advocating for a better ethic among those who follow Him.

Certainly, the Pharisees (Jewish religious leaders of Jesus' time) would have had the whole *thirst after righteousness* down – at least in the sense they understood righteousness to be. But this? Be merciful? They would have failed daily, because being merciful is to take on a posture toward others that acknowledges their value as a human being as the same, or even more, than yourself, and then acting on that belief with compassion. Jesus tells a story to illustrate what being merciful looks like. The story is known as "The Good Samaritan," where a man is left for dead on the side of the road, two religious leaders pass him by in fear of becoming unclean, but a Samaritan approaches the dying man. The Samaritan has compassion for the man and decides to take a posture of mercy. So, in response to this, he takes care of the man and restores him to full health. This is the key in Jesus' desire for His followers to be merciful – that we wouldn't only think mercifully, but we would act mercifully.

As we move closer to the last few characteristics, we'll see that this characteristic, like the others, is one that is lived out today, but the promise will ultimately be realized when we come into the new kingdom. But this shouldn't deter us from living mercifully, for we are people who embody God's kingdom here and now. The place we live – this world – will *not* be merciful back to us, but that doesn't change our path. We walk this way regardless of consequence, for we have been transformed for a purpose that transcends this world and enters eternity.

*"Blessed are the pure in heart, for they shall see God" (Matthew 5:8).* As I write this, the official start of winter is only a month and a half away. It's the general time of the year where I begin to start my car in the cold with anticipation to leave right away for work, but then realize that my windshield is completely frosted or iced over. If I leave right away, I would surely run into something because I wouldn't be able to see through the windshield. So, I do what I need to do – sometimes – to get the windshield to the point where I have a small gap of visibility – don't lie, you know you've done this too – and usually by the time I get to the main road, I can see much better.

Imagine this... You went mudding in your awesome Jeep. Your windshield was completely caked with a few inches thick of mud. Instead of cleaning the mud off, you decide to drive home like Jim Carrey on *Ace Ventura: Pet Detective* (if you don't get the reference, look it up). You pull into your driveway, and then you go into your house to clean yourself up. The next morning you go outside, expectant to leave for work in that same Jeep, but quickly realize that you're not going anywhere for a while. Your windshield is now not only caked with a few inches of mud, but now it is covered with a few inches of ice on top of that. You wouldn't be able see anything through that windshield. So, what do you do? You begin to chip away at the problem.

This is simply a picture of what an impure heart looks like. It's dirty, grimy, and past the point where you can clean it yourself. With an impure heart, you will not see God. You can't. But thankfully, Christ is the heart purifier, and it is He who cleanses us of the mud and muck that wrap our hearts without Him. Sin has deeply damaged the human heart, and it is only Christ who can purify it. And the promise is that with a purified heart, we will one day *see* God. The One whom we have believed will be visible to us in some way. And since we approach His throne covered by Christ's blood, we can approach His throne with reverent confidence. What a promise that is!

*"Blessed are the peacemakers, for they shall be called sons of God" (Matthew 5:9).* As Jesus is saying this, you're sitting

there wondering what your buddy Simon the Zealot is thinking. Simon is a guy who is all about a political revolution in his nation. Depending on your vantage point, Simon is either a patriotic militia member or a grass-roots terrorist. He doesn't like that the Romans are ruling over Israel, and he wants them out, like yesterday. But the amazing thing about Simon the Zealot is that he is following this Rabbi who is teaching him to be merciful and to be a peacemaker. Does Jesus only mean to be merciful and a peacemaker toward his own people?

There is a peace spectrum where all of us reside somewhere between two opposing ends. On one end, there are the passive head-in-the-sand dwellers. These people don't *ever* want to rock the boat. Under no circumstances will they go against the grain. And from the outside, they seem like the peaceful people in our midst. They go along with what the majority wants and are simply happy if everyone else is happy. On another end, there are the aggressive revolutionaries of resolution. These people don't *ever* want tension to go unresolved. They approach conflict in a different way. They see *rocking the boat* as the only way to resolve misunderstandings and conflicts. They do not waste any time in addressing concerns and frustrations. Both types of people represent extremes on a scale we all are on. You and I tend to lean toward one end or the other. You may even be one of the most extreme of ends. So, which end is best? Which tactic makes peace?

If you want to be a peacemaker, you must fight for balance on this scale. You must not be the borderline cowardly who will run from the first sign of conflict, and you must not be the borderline bully who will run toward the first sign of conflict. However, you still must deal with conflict if you want to be a peacemaker. Personally, I lean toward the bully end of the scale, but I am learning that tact is quite helpful. Sometimes, to make peace, we must show all sides of the situation where they have gone right and where they have gone wrong. To make peace, we must be proactive in bringing it about, but not in a way so aggressive that we do more harm than good. In fact, when we take on the title of peacemaker and live accordingly, we are following our Savior, a.k.a. the Prince of Peace.

*"Blessed are those who are persecuted for righteousness' sake, for theirs is the kingdom of heaven" (Matthew 5:10).* Let's cut straight to the chase. Neither the enemy nor the world he rules over desires for you to live into your reality as one who has been crucified to life. He knows that when you not only understand who you are now – that you are rescued, restored, renewed, and indwelled by God's Spirit – but also when you live into who you are, you will wreak havoc on his mission. He knows this and he wants to

deter you from God's mission. He doesn't want you to live righteously. He doesn't want you to be merciful, to be a peacemaker, to be any of this, because he knows that you will be an example of the antithesis of what he wants people to be.

Know this: we must stay the course and see setbacks, criticisms, and persecutions as a sign that we are blessed by God. If we begin to believe that God's plan for our lives only includes rainbows, success, roses, happiness, butterflies, and prosperity, then we are believing a lie from the evil one. He wants us to believe this because it will deter us from being those who have been crucified to life. It will encourage us to bend to culture's view of things. It will entice us to always try to paint the hard truths of Scripture as now irrelevant. It will cause us to retreat when God wants us to advance.

The linchpin on persecution, however, is that the reason for us being persecuted is for righteousness' sake. This means that we *must* live into who God has crucified us to be. This means we must lead with love and hold to both grace *and* truth. This does not mean that we should look for opportunities to be persecuted, but rather should look for opportunities to live out our identity in Christ. And notice the promise in His statement. It's the same as where we started. But wait. There's one more characteristic Jesus gives to drive His point home deep into our hearts.

*"Blessed are you when others revile you and persecute you and utter all kinds of evil against you falsely on my account. Rejoice and be glad, for your reward is great in heaven, for so they persecuted the prophets who were before you." (Matthew 5:11-12).* Imagine the temperature of the group as Jesus speaks these words. Crowds are flocking toward Him as He tells you that you will be blessed when others revile you, speak evil against you, and persecute you. Look around. The beautiful scenery is beginning to seem less and less beautiful. What you understand about God's blessings is beginning to be transformed. It's almost as if you're not quite sure what to think anymore. And to think, this is only Jesus' introduction to His sermon on the mountainside!

Heirs of the kingdom of heaven aren't overcome by this kingdom. Instead, they see their present troubles as incomparable to the blessings of what is to come in the near future. Like a military leader, training up another group of recruits, Jesus is preparing His followers for what will come for them and, even before that, what will come for Him. And that's the beauty of Jesus' message. He is not calling us to go where He is not willing to go Himself, for He was destined to go much further than any of us can go.

Jesus paved the way for our reward in heaven because He was willing to go down and defeat the enemy so that we all can have a piece of the victory. And it is this future hope that propels us past our present circumstances and allows us to rejoice and be glad when trouble comes. We are heirs to the kingdom of heaven. And as heirs, we walk in this kingdom to the beat of a different drum than all the rest. We walk to the beat of God's blessings – we are anomalies for God's glory.

## A Radically Different Way

In 2016, Lifeway Research and Ligonier Ministries partnered together to conduct a major piece of research called, *The State of Theology*. They set out to determine what Americans believe about God, sin, and other important topics of theology. One frightening statistic they found was that 73 percent of Americans disagreed strongly or disagreed somewhat with this statement: "Even the smallest sin deserves eternal damnation." It's frightening to me in particular, because the majority of Americans do, in fact, believe in God. Since they believe in God but don't believe that He takes even small sins seriously, they misunderstand not only God's holiness and Christ's sacrifice, but also their need for forgiveness.

When we say that small sins are not really that serious to God, we are blatantly disagreeing with Jesus Himself (as well as the entire account of Scripture, from beginning to end). To see this clearly, let's go back to the scenic situation where Jesus is preaching to His disciples. Put yourself back in the place of one of His disciples. Get comfortable because Jesus has more to say and more things that will completely change your mind.

Many people want to completely throw out the Old Testament, as if it is irrelevant and outdated. Jesus didn't do that, and neither did the apostles who preached and taught after His ascension. Like us Americans, many Jews had begun misunderstanding how God sees sin. In response to this, Jesus says these words to His disciples (and to us):

> For truly, I say to you, until heaven and earth pass away, not an iota, not a dot, will pass from the Law until all is accomplished. [19] Therefore whoever relaxes one of the least of these commandments and teaches others to do the same will be called least in the kingdom of heaven, but whoever does them and teaches them will be called great in the kingdom of heaven. – Matthew 5:18-19

After saying this, He begins to drill down into specific types of sin to show a radically different way of living and understanding sin. Jesus' way is so radically different that you'll be tempted to disagree with Him. In fact, most people will disagree with Him. We'll be tempted to judge what He says based on our own sense of justice and righteousness. But we need to fight that temptation because Jesus never concedes to *our* sense of justice and righteousness. We'll want to fight back with our own logic, but we must see, at the outset, that God's way is the only way. And as the crucified, we are empowered to follow His way.

In each of the following sections, we'll see the radically different way that heirs to the kingdom of heaven are called to.

## Anger?

Let's imagine for a moment that you have a sibling. And let's suppose that there's a situation that your sibling handles poorly. What's your reaction? If you do, in fact, have a sibling you know what it is right away. *You big dummy! Are you a fool or something? What in the world were you thinking?!* Sound about right? If you don't have a sibling, just go with it. Not a big deal, right? Wrong. At least according to Jesus.

Jesus uses a similar story as an example as to how murder results in the same judgment as an insult. And yes, you read that correctly. Jesus leveled the field between murder and insult. Obviously on a here-and-now level, murder is more extreme. But that's not Jesus' point. He's speaking to young Jewish men who were taught the Torah, the first five books of the Old Testament. They understood God's commands – at least they thought they did.

Jesus isn't concerned about our logic and our rationalizations. He is concerned with transforming our hearts and minds. Let His words sink in:

> everyone who is angry with his brother will be liable to judgment; whoever insults his brother will be liable to the council; and whoever says, 'You fool!' will be liable to the hell of fire. – Matthew 5:22.

Let's say that you got a sizeable bonus at work, and since you're excited about investing in God's kingdom, you decide to give half of that bonus to your local church. At the same time, a few days earlier, you and a coworker got into an argument that turned personal. Insults were thrown from either side, and there was never a point of reconciliation afterward. So, with that being the situation, should you give that sizeable gift to your local church? You may be wondering what the connection is. Consider Jesus' words:

> So if you are offering your gift at the altar and there remember that your brother has something against you, [24] leave your gift there before the altar and go.

First be reconciled to your brother, and then come and offer your gift. – Matthew 5:23-24

As an heir to the kingdom of heaven, you are to operate under a different set of standards than the laws of the land that will punish you for murder but let you slide on some anger. Jesus is showing us that His concern begins with what is in our hearts. Every outward act of evil first manifests itself in the heart of its culprit. If there is anger in your heart that transforms into hate, it has already crossed the line into sin.

Imagine what it would look like to do everything you could to reconcile relational wrongs. Imagine being able to go to bed at night knowing that you sought healing where there was brokenness. Imagine the immense amount of peace you would feel as you go before God, confident that you have done what is right in His eyes. It's possible, but it requires a deep dedication to following Christ, the Prince of Peace. Because without that deep dedication to Him, we'll continue to hold grudges and speak gossip, for both are a result of pride and self-centeredness. And that, my friend, is not who you are anymore. Christ has taken you from selfish to selfless, from prideful to humble.

## Lust?

Jesus doesn't stop at pushing against our assumptions with anger and murder. He goes to hot button number two: adultery. Now, you may be thinking, *good, I haven't done that*; but not so fast. Jesus knows His audience. He knows that you know that adultery is wrong, but He also knows that we – you and I – aren't as slick as we think we are. Just look at these words: "everyone who looks at a woman with lustful intent has already committed adultery with her in his heart" (Matthew 5:28).

Let's make things uncomfortable, shall we? 64 percent of American men report that they view pornography at least monthly.[4] Ladies, you're not immune; 33 percent of all visits to adult websites come from women.[5] Lustful intent is kind of the point of pornography, isn't it?

To make things even worse, pornography isn't a required component for looking at a woman with lustful intent. Go anywhere and the possibility is there. And it doesn't stop there. Images from the past can easily be prompted in the mind. Lust can occur anywhere, anytime, especially when you've given yourself to it multiple times over your lifetime.

---

[4] Stats from https://www.xxxchurch.com/stats/men

[5] Stats from https://www.xxxchurch.com/stats/women

Jesus' call to action is quite frightening. Cut out or cut off that which is causing you to sin. If your eyes are causing you to sin, gouge them out. If your hand is causing you to sin, cut it off. His rationale? "For it is better that you lose one of your members than that your whole body go into hell" (Matthew 5:30b). In other words, sin is serious – even the sin that happens in your heart and mind.

Thankfully for us, we understand two things when looking at Jesus' words: first, Jesus is using hyperbole to make His point, and second, He has made the way for us to be cleansed from our sins.

So, as heirs to the kingdom of heaven, we operate from an understanding that what we think is just as important as what we do. We know that what we do flows from what we know and think. And we take heart, for Christ has made us new and is transforming our minds to His way of thinking and living. Instead of giving in to the temptation of looking at someone with lustful intent, we fight that temptation and begin to see them as someone made in the image of God – as someone who should be honored and respected, not objectified.

## Divorce?

I know, I know. It seems like the sensitive issues don't stop. I understand that this is a touchy subject for many in our world today. But it's a part of this conversation because Jesus followed His teaching on adultery with His teaching on divorce. Are you still there with Him on the scenic mountainside? At this point He's probably a little over five minutes into His sermon and He's doing something that only He can do: He is making everyone mad at the same time. Of course, it's not for the sake of simply making people mad, but for the sake of reorienting our minds toward the way of the crucified, toward the way of the kingdom of heaven.

Jesus continues His pattern of acknowledging what has been taught to His disciples: "It was also said, 'Whoever divorces his wife, let him give her a certificate of divorce'" (Matthew 5:31). It's that simple: give your spouse a certificate letting her know that you want a divorce. Kind of like *divorce papers* today that are drawn up by lawyers and signed by couples to end the covenant relationship they entered before God, family, and friends. But just because that is what was told to the Jews who wanted a divorce, it doesn't make divorce right.

Here's what Jesus says is going on when someone gets a divorce:

> But I say to you that everyone who divorces his wife, except on the ground of sexual immorality, makes her

commit adultery, and whoever marries a divorced woman commits adultery. – Matthew 5:32

There is one acceptable ground for divorce and that is sexual immorality. Otherwise, the wife is led into adultery and the man commits the same sin by leading her there. It's important to note that during the first Century it was normal for only the man to be able to initiate a divorce. Obviously today our dynamic is different; it's normal for a divorce to be initiated by the man or the woman.

To Jesus, marriage is a covenantal relationship. In other words, it is a relationship that two enter, and the only way for it to be broken – truly broken – is for the man or the woman to die. With marriage being liked to God's relationship with His Church, aren't we glad that He isn't going to simply present us with a certificate saying that He wants to end His relationship with us?! The relationship between He and His Church is deeper than that, as is the marriage relationship. It is not to be entered lightly and is to remain for life.

## Retaliate?

In our day and time Jesus' teaching, often referred to as "turn the other cheek," is the most ignored. It is often responded to with rebuttals and elaborate justifications for where it doesn't apply. Without a doubt, this is one that easily gets under our skin, and certainly would have with Jesus' disciples as they sat and listened to Him teach it. They may have gotten up and walked away if they knew what was in store for their futures.

Jesus took their sense of personal justice and flipped it on its head:

> You have heard that it was said, 'An eye for an eye and a tooth for a tooth.'[39] But I say to you, do not resist the one who is evil. But if anyone slaps you on the right cheek, turn to him the other also. – Matthew 5:38-39

Every single teaching I've heard on this passage *immediately*, upon reading it, goes into a full description of all the different situations where Jesus would be okay for us to not follow His teaching here. I do not know of any other New Testament teaching that is approached with such cold feet and caution. If we would begin to reflect on this passage with full confidence that Jesus did intend for us to follow what He taught, we would begin to better understand His entire sermon on the mountainside.

But this begs a question… Why? Why would Jesus tell us to allow ourselves to be in harm's way longer than we need to be? This is a passage of Scripture that I have wrestled with ever since I first read it. Being a naïve and new Christ follower, I took Jesus seriously, and in doing so, I began understanding the way of Jesus in what I thought was more of a complete picture. But then I was dumbfounded by the number of Christians who didn't respond to this passage with the same application. Instead of hearing a radical adoption of the principle behind it, I began hearing justification after justification as to how this didn't apply to most situations – they never used the word 'most,' but their descriptions surely arrived there.

So, why? My hope is that it's clear to you, but then again, I don't doubt if it's still fuzzy. The reason isn't because you're not super spiritual or that you're trying to avoid the way of the crucified; the reason this passage is still fuzzy is likely because it goes against *everything* we have ever been taught and *everything* we have ever taught our kids. Jesus isn't concerned with what human logic tells us regarding this matter; He is simply continuing the process of transforming our minds and hearts toward His ways and His kingdom ethic. For those of us who have been rescued, renewed, transformed, and indwelled by the very Spirit of God, we are called to a radically different way of life. A life of meekness.

One of the characteristics we saw earlier for those who are heirs to the kingdom of heaven is this frightening word: meekness. Those who are meek are blessed and heirs to the new earth. We don't like the word, let alone the implications, because we have been taught that confidence and assertiveness are requirements for being successful in this world. But what Jesus is showing us throughout His entire sermon is that those who follow Him are those who adopt His same attitude and approach to life. In other words, they see their lives as the vessels for living out their mission and are not as concerned about themselves as they are about others.

Who are the most likely people to strike you in the face? I remember a pastor by the name of Perry Noble say this simple, yet truth-filled statement: "hurt people hurt people." We know this to be true when it comes to bullies on the playground and adults who chase strife. Those who hurt others are hurting, and Jesus is showing us that our concern should be for the hurting person more than the safety of ourselves.

This truth is deeply connected to Jesus' next teaching point. And yes, I know, Jesus doesn't give much time for us to take a breath. He goes from one hard truth to another. Feel free to pause and reflect.

## Enemies?

I can find out anything noteworthy with the tip of my finger.

We all can if we have a smartphone. We can all see the violence that plagues the world. We can see terrorist groups rising up, persecuting and killing Christians. We can see hatred of all shapes and sizes. We can watch shootings and murders on video – real ones. We can see videos of beheadings online. The violence of our day, whether it's more than in the past or not, is at our finger tips.

This opens the door to more opportunities for hatred. Everything in us tells us that hating evil is okay. But then Jesus screws that up for us too. Just look at what He says:

> You have heard that it was said, 'You shall love your neighbor and hate your enemy.' But I say to you, Love your enemies and pray for those who persecute you. – Matthew 5:43-44

While we immediately want to objectify those who are our enemies, Jesus reminds us of their humanity. What we are called to is not hatred toward them, but love and prayer toward them. And then Jesus drops this bomb on His disciples, and on us:

> For if you love those who love you, what reward do you have? Do not even the tax collectors do the same? [47] And if you greet only your brothers, what more are you doing than others? Do not even the Gentiles do the same? [48] You therefore must be perfect, as your heavenly Father is perfect. – Matthew 5:46-48

Picture this: again, you're sitting there listening to Jesus teach, and then suddenly, He calls out the tax collector in your midst, Matthew. He turns red and nods affirmatively: *yes, we do love those who love us*. But to ensure no one is left out, He calls all of you out and puts you on the same level as the Gentiles. You're offended and hurt, but you see His point. And then He says that little statement about being perfect. You begin thinking to yourself, as you are now, *I'm not perfect, nor can I ever hope to be*.

## Perfection

All this time, Jesus has been teaching about the kingdom of heaven and about those who are heirs to that kingdom. He goes into hot-button topic after hot-button topic and describes a radical way of going about life. It's not radical in that it's boisterous; it's radical because it's entirely different from the norm. He is, in a powerful way, describing what it means to be an anomaly for God's glory. And then at the end, He reminds us of a foundational truth as to what it means to be a follower of His.

Most of the time, maybe even all of the time, when we see the word 'perfect' we think of something that is without fault. Another way of understanding perfection, though, is by thinking of completeness. And I believe both meanings are in order here. First, a follower of

Christ is to be perfect as the Lord, our Heavenly Father, is perfect in the sense that we are to be without fault. This can only be accomplished through the blood of Christ and only realized when He returns to bring us into the kingdom He has been telling us about. Second, a follower of Christ is to be perfect as the Lord, our Heavenly Father, is perfect in the sense that every part of us is to be completely conformed to His ways. Our motivations, then, are completely subordinate to His motivations.

## LET THE BEAT DROP

The beat that we live by is that of an heir to the kingdom of heaven, and Jesus has just laid out what that looks like. The beat is different from what most people are used to, but that's to be expected. We will go against the grain of common sense, and people won't understand why. But, that's part of being an anomaly. We deviate from what is expected and take on a path that is much less traveled.

The way of the crucified isn't easy, but we are not on the journey by ourselves. Christ is here with us, guiding us, walking with us, and paving the way – all at the same time. This is His present work, for it has never stopped. We will surely stumble at times, but we must get back up and go on, we must. This is what we do; this is who we are. We are anomalies for God's glory.

CHAPTER 7

# MATTERS OF THE HEART

*While you are proclaiming peace with your lips, be careful to have it even more fully in your heart. — Saint Francis of Assisi*

I'll just come out and say it: the fall season is the best season of the year. Growing up, the fall season was a steady dose of football, getting back to school, hockey, Halloween, my birthday, Thanksgiving, and even more football. One particular fall season specifically sticks out in my mind. It was the year that my wife and I began dating. It was my junior year of high school and her sophomore year. Our first date together was to the Haunted Cave in Fort Wayne, Indiana. I mean, what better date would ensure the ability to hold her hand and be the brave knight amid a hostile environment? Let's just say that she had no chance – she was going to fall in love with me for sure.

As we were standing in line, there were a few characters sneaking behind everyone who was waiting to get in. And as our place in line crept toward the door, we began noticing signs that read, *BEWARE*. Following that frightening word was a description of what was in store for anyone and everyone who dared to walk in the doors of the Haunted Cave. We knew, in some sense, what we were getting ourselves into.

Looking back at my childhood, these *BEWARE* signs pop up in a multitude of places. They were posted on fences warning people that a dog was present. They were posted along the dirt bike trail me and my friends frequented, warning people that the railroad didn't allow trespassers. We ignored the signs. They were posted at the entrance of a warehouse of a local business where my friend's mom worked. We ignored the signs. *BEWARE* signs are important to pay attention to even though we often don't.

## Beware of Where Your Heart is

Let's take a moment to refresh the scene we explored in the last chapter. Jesus and His disciples are on a mountainside. Jesus is preaching and teaching His disciples while the crowds are likely at the foot of the mountain. Picturing yourself as one of the disciples, you look around at the breathtaking view. But even that view can't keep you from hearing Jesus say surprising statement after surprising statement and then continue to explain and show what an heir to the kingdom of heaven is like. And now, Jesus continues His teaching with this statement: "Beware of practicing your righteousness before other people in order to be seen by them, for then you will have no reward from your Father who is in heaven" (Matthew 6:1).

On one hand, Jesus says that His followers are the light of the world, yet on the other hand, Jesus says that His followers are to abstain from seeking the spotlight. They are the light, but they are not to be in the spotlight. Instead, the light is to be aimed at the One who is the source of the light.

Let's be honest, this is hard. We live in a time where we can broadcast every little thing we do, and many of us do just that. I'm surely guilty. It's odd to do something worthwhile and *not* share it with the world. Not only that, but we share something with the world and then we want to make sure people "like" it or "love" it or maybe even "haha" it. Or maybe that's just me.

Now, I'm not saying that social media is wrong or bad. What I am saying is that it is a possible vehicle for us to "practice our righteousness" before others in hopes that we'll be seen by them. The ultimate desire is to not just be seen by people for the sake of being seen, but that others would think better of, or even admire, us.

Whenever we take the time to document and broadcast the good things we do, posting them for all to see, we must beware of our motive. Is it the spotlight we are seeking or is it the light we are seeking to share? That's the difference. The spotlight is given by man and only magnifies our part. The light that is given by God is simply there to reflect attention back to the One on the throne.

We are light-bearers for the glory of God, not ourselves. We do good because we are called to and because He allows us to. We don't get to take credit for any of the good things we do. He is the One doing them through us, and He is the One who planned for us to do them in the first place. Our hearts must be in a look-at-Him place rather than a look-at-me place. The difference is subtle and it's not always clear from the outside.

## Door Number One or Door Number Two?

Do you like game shows? I used to love watching *The Price is Right*. Let's suppose that you are the person who yells, "One dollar!" to the frustration of the rest of the contestants, and you win. As you arrive on the stage of the iconic game show, you greet Drew Carey – I know, you probably prefer Bob Barker. You now get the chance to play a game for some prizes. Let's call the game, "Two Doorways." Drew proceeds to explain to you that behind door number one is an eternal reward, and behind door number two is a reward equivalent to five minutes of fame. Which doorway do you decide to go through?

I know, the game is quite uneventful since you already know the *kind* of reward you'll get with each doorway, but this is no different from life with Christ. This is basically what He is teaching to the disciples on the mountainside. If you want to do good for the sake of the spotlight, the spotlight is your only reward. Just look at this:

> Thus, when you give to the needy, sound no trumpet before you, as the hypocrites do in the synagogues and in the streets, that they may be praised by others. Truly, I say to you, they have received their reward. – Matthew 6:2

The best examples the disciples had for what it meant to be godly people were the people Jesus called hypocrites in the synagogues. These hypocrites were the religious leaders of the first century. And so, Jesus points them away from those examples and toward a heart that is after God's glory. Those religious leaders surely cared about pleasing God, but in the midst of their good deeds, they made the decision to flaunt it before others in hopes of being noticed. And of course, the implication is that they *were* noticed, and thus, they received their only reward: human recognition.

## AN AUDIENCE OF ONE

Jesus had seen it before. People would give money away to those in need. People would pray lofty, eloquent prayers. The money was given in such a way that it could easily be known to others. The prayers were designed to impress the onlookers and fellow participants. And let's not act as though these same occasions aren't potential opportunities for us to fall into pride as well.

We're human beings living in a world of sin; we can certainly turn any good thing into the antithesis of what Jesus desires for us. If we are the most generous of all and the most thoughtful pray-ers, it means nothing if our audience is more than one. If we are using these good and righteous acts as vehicles to fish for compliments and praise, we are not worshiping the One True God; we are worshiping ourselves.

Jesus tells us we are to give and pray in secret. He calls us to a life of losing ourselves for the sake of the glorification of His name. We are not our own anymore; we are His. Completely His. And when we allow ourselves to fall into prideful generosity and praying, we allow Satan to creep into our lives in the most subtle and powerful way.

This is exactly what the enemy wants for Christ followers. He wants us to believe we are living for and worshiping God with our lives while we simultaneously lift ourselves up – high and exalted. This is exactly why Jesus tells us to "not let your left hand know what your right hand is doing" (Matthew 6:3b) when we give to those who are in need. It's exactly why He tells us to "go into your room and shut the door and pray to your Father who is in secret. And your Father who sees in secret will reward you" (Matthew 6:6). Nothing we do will go unnoticed because our audience of One can see everything, everywhere, always.

## Beware of This Prayer

My high school football team prayed a particular prayer every Friday night before our game. I had no idea what the words were, but many of my teammates did. The problem was, many (probably most) of us didn't really understand what we were praying. At least looking back, that's what it seemed like to me.

As I have followed Christ longer and longer, I have come to realize that what is popularly known as "The Lord's Prayer" is quite intense and is far beyond something to just recite. So, pray this if you will, but beware of what you are saying, for if sincerely prayed and sincerely followed, The Lord's Prayer may lead to your life looking completely different today than it did yesterday.

Jesus is so kind to us. He tells us we ought not pray a bunch of empty phrases when we communicate with God, and at the same time, shows us *how* to pray instead. Specifically, He tells us to "pray then like this" (Matthew 6:9a), which means we can use this as a model for how we can pray in an honorable way. We don't need to simply recite the same words as we always do, for that runs the risk of becoming rote recitation instead of sincere communication. With that in mind, let's see the prayer that Jesus tells us to use as our model, one line at a time.

*"Our Father in heaven, hallowed be your name" (Matthew 6:9b).* Notice the heart behind this. We address God with the intimate name of Father. He is our Almighty, perfect Father who has a desire to be looked at as such. In Christ, we are sons and daughters of His. Our relationship is an intimate father-daughter/father-son dynamic. We can go to Him for comfort, for guidance, for providence, for everything. And we can go to Him with confidence and security. As we address Him as Father, we are also asking Him to make His name holy – set apart and exalted. While we confide in Him as our Father, we are acknowledging His holiness, reverence, and our call to glorify His name.

*"Your kingdom come, your will be done, on earth as it is in heaven" (Matthew 6:10).* The kingdom of heaven is both a present reality and a future hope. It is a present reality, because as heirs to the kingdom, we are here with Christ in us. It is our future hope, because it will be fully manifested when Christ returns to make all things complete and new. And so, our prayer is that God's kingdom would come and His will be done *here* as it is *there*. Those who have been crucified with Christ have also been raised with Christ, thus, we are vessels of His kingdom and tools of His will. And so, we pray this truth and this desire, for His kingdom is coming and, at the same time, it is here. His will has been manifested through Jesus and is continuing to be done through the Spirit in us.

*"Give us this day our daily bread" (Matthew 6:11).* Our Father is our Sovereign Provider. Everything that we have is His. Our food, our shelter, our family, our friends, our clothes, our money, our transportation – these are all His. The breath in our lungs, the blood in our veins, the purpose in our heart, the joy in our soul – these are all His. Nothing we have is our own. We are blessed to receive from the Provider of all good and perfect things. He holds the Universe together. It's by His grace that we exist, and it is with that understanding that we ask Him for our daily bread and our daily needs.

*"And forgive us our debts, as we also have forgiven our debtors"* *(Matthew 6:12).* This one almost feels like a bait-and-switch statement, doesn't it? Lord, forgive me. No. Forgive me as I have also forgiven. In other words, we must follow our Father in love toward others, and a big part of that is our willingness and proactivity to forgive others. Our Heavenly Father is and has been willing to be proactive in creating the opportunity to forgive us. We should also be willing to forgive others and be proactive in giving them the opportunity to receive our forgiveness.

*"And lead us not into temptation, but deliver us from evil"* *(Matthew 6:13).* We can be confident that if we end up in an evil place, it is not because our Father led us there. Our Father doesn't lead us into temptation; He leads us out of temptation. He is our Rescuer from the evil we get ourselves into. Jesus knows that we will mess up and give in to temptation, but He doesn't want us to forget who our Deliverer is.

Do you see the underlying posture and beliefs in that prayer? Jesus' model for prayer both reminds us of God's grace as well as our need for it. His model for prayer both reminds us of God's nature as well as our new nature as His sons and daughters. This prayer is for those who are heirs to the kingdom of heaven, for it is a daily reminder of our destiny and our devotion. Beware of this prayer.

You may just find that through it, you will better understand your Father and your place in His kingdom.

## A Test of Heart

My oldest daughter is an attention-to-detail type of person. She's three. So get this: one day we were relaxing on the recliner in our living room, when suddenly one of the bulbs in our ceiling fan decided to cease from living out its purpose. It was done, and she noticed right away. She proceeded to exclaim, "daddy, daddy, look over there!" As I turned my gaze from her excited face to the dead bulb in our light fixture, I realized this could be a teachable moment.

Now please understand, parenting is hard. I'm sure I miss most opportunities for teachable moments. I often feel as though I'm just doing trial and error when it comes to parenting my two little girls. But thankfully, this was one of those moments that I noticed. If it stuck or not, well that's another story.

As her attention was fixated on the light fixture, I began to answer her *why is it like that* question with a detailed examination of the worth of things in this world. We explored their dependability, our limitations as creators of things, and our need to put our hope and our hearts in the things that don't pass away – the things of heaven, the things of God. I was feeling pretty good about my little teaching until she looked back at me and asked, "but why?" I chuckled and tried explaining again. Eventually the questions of "why?" stopped and we continued on with our day.

The question my daughter asked is a question we take for granted. When she saw something that we replace often stop working, she asked a foundational question: why? Why do the things of this world stop working so often? Why is it that we can't create anything that lasts? Or better yet, why do we put so much of our time, energy, and money toward things that give us negative returns? But this isn't simply a question of economics; it's a question of purpose. If all we devote our lives to is the accumulation of things that pass away, then what kind of purpose are we living?

I don't know what the line is for you, the line that goes from necessity to luxury in terms of your way of life. The light bulb is replaced, of course. We have a home, transportation, and all our basic needs met, and then some. But that's not the end of the story for us, and hopefully it's not the end of the story for you either, especially considering these words straight from Jesus:

> Do not lay up for yourselves treasures on earth, where moth and rust destroy and where thieves break in and steal, [20] but lay up for yourselves treasures in

heaven, where neither moth nor rust destroys and where thieves do not break in and steal. [21] For where your treasure is, there your heart will be also. – Matthew 6:19-21

Wherever your treasure goes, your heart goes. So, where are they both going? Early in my walk with God, I didn't understand this. I didn't understand generosity and supporting God's mission financially. They say the last thing to be sanctified in a person is his or her wallet. I wholeheartedly agree. And make no mistake, Jesus is clear that the treasure leads the heart. If we haven't surrendered our treasure, we haven't really surrendered our hearts.

To be sure that Jesus was, in fact, speaking on money and not some other "asset," He clarifies by saying, "No one can serve two masters, for either he will hate the one and love the other, or he will be devoted to the one and despise the other. You cannot serve God and money" (Matthew 6:24). The way of the crucified is the way of *one* Master, not multiple masters. And when we refuse to give up control of our finances, we are refusing to give up control to Christ.

Like I said before, my family has a home, transportation, and all our needs met, and more. But what we have done beyond that is we have made a commitment to biblical generosity. Once we began to understand what Jesus was calling us to in terms of how to use our treasures, it was clear to us. We decided to start with the tithe and go up from there. To be clear, a tithe is simply a tenth. So, we started with an amount equal to ten percent of our household income, before taxes, and set that aside to give back to God. We have increased our giving beyond that as well, but the point is, God is calling all of us to use our treasures for His purposes, His mission, and His kingdom.

There's a temptation in this world to keep up with the Joneses. It may be cliché, but clichés are such for a reason – they represent reality. We probably all need to be reminded that the only audience that counts is the audience of One, the One on the throne of the Universe. We can spend all our lives trying to impress our neighbors with the next best thing, or we can seek to love and lead our neighbors to the ultimate best: God Himself.

As always, whenever the money conversation comes up, this disclaimer comes out: money is not evil. The love of money is the root of all kinds of evil. It's the love that we have for our treasure that's the problem. In the same vein, nice things aren't evil, but the love of them is the root of all kinds of evil. Your "stuff" isn't the problem, but when your heart begins to follow your "stuff" rather than Christ, *Houston, we have a problem!*

At the same time, that disclaimer is kind of misleading in light of what Jesus is saying. He doesn't address whether the treasure is evil or not. Instead, He makes the case that the location of the treasure is the deciding factor. So, let's take this further. If the location of your treasure is found in the various numbers that make up your bank account and the things that can be acquired from it, then there's a problem. In other words, if your treasure is found in the economy of this kingdom rather than the economy of the kingdom of heaven, your heart is in the wrong location. If your treasure is in the economy of this kingdom, your treasure will be made up of paper and coins with people's faces on them. If your treasure is in the economy of the kingdom of heaven, your treasure will be made up of lived-out, Christ-centered love.

In order to have your treasure truly in the right place, your heart has to be following the *right thing*. Is your heart oriented toward God's mission and your place in it, or is it oriented toward the lavish opportunities of this world? How you use your money says everything about where your treasure truly is and where your heart truly resides.

When we begin to grasp the joy of having our treasure in the things of God, we'll begin to understand what it means to live for an audience of One. This is the way of the crucified. This is the abundant life. Shift the focus from self to God and others.

## A Test of Trust

Recently, my wife went to the grocery store for a "big haul" as she would call it. I stayed home with our girls. Hmm, yes, the grocery store. It's a concept we all understand and have grown accustomed to. It's genius, really. Food of all kinds, in one place, for sale, for all to come and purchase. Have you ever thought of what you would do if you didn't have a grocery store? I have. And, let's just say it's not a reassuring thought. In fact, the thought brings about some worry in me. I've never been interested in fishing. I've never gone hunting. I've never had to prepare an animal to be cooked. (By this I mean handling every stage from live animal to dinner plate). I've never grown a garden – well, unless you count helping my great grandmother with hers when I was five years old, but really, she did all the work and I was just company. I would be lost. Worried. Anxious.

While they certainly had markets in the first century that provided an opportunity kind of like a grocery store, food on the table, clothes on your back, and water to drink weren't as available then as they are today. Whether basic needs were met or not had to surely cause anxiety and worry for many in the first century. And I know, making sure basic needs are met causes a lot of people anxiety and worry today as well. Just because the grocery store is on the corner doesn't mean that everyone has a way to pay for the groceries they need.

Consider that, directly following His statement that we cannot serve God *and* money, Jesus says this:

> Therefore I tell you, do not be anxious about your life, what you will eat or what you will drink, nor about your body, what you will put on. Is not life more than food, and the body more than clothing? – Matthew 6:25

Remember Jesus' audience? He is speaking to His disciples who left businesses, homes, families, and ways of life to follow Him. They were living as people with no home. They didn't know where their next meal was going to come from. They didn't know if they would have clothes on their backs, especially considering that Jesus told them that they should be willing to give up their tunic if someone asked for it. Can you imagine? Of course they were worried and anxious about life. They were living on the edge with the Rabbi who called them to follow Him wherever He went.

In the same way, consider yourself and your present situation. What would Jesus tell you to not worry and be anxious about? Is it your finances? Your children? Your marriage? Your friendships? Your career? Your diagnosis? The unknown? Everything? What causes you to be troubled? No matter what it is, Jesus says this to His disciples and to you: "And which of you by being anxious can add a single hour to his span of life?" (Matthew 6:27).

Living abundant life in Christ does not mean you get a pass on difficulties and things that will cause you to worry. Instead, it provides you a perspective that will help you persevere *through* the difficulties. For the disciples, Jesus reminded them that God is their provider. While they were worried about food, He pointed them to the birds who neither plant nor harvest. While they were worried about clothing, He pointed them to lilies that were clothed beautifully even though they were not spun into existence. Jesus spoke directly to their worries and their anxieties. And I believe He is speaking to you today. He is speaking directly to your worries and your anxieties, pointing you to the bigger picture of His purposes. Are you listening?

## Jesus' Bottom Line

Here's the bottom line that Jesus gave His disciples and the bottom line He is giving to you today: "But seek first the kingdom of God and his righteousness, and all these things will be added to you" (Matthew 6:33). The solution to anxiety and worry is the same as what it means to have your treasure in the right place. It is all connected. All of it. When we live for an audience of One, our finances are propelled to a place of purpose. When our finances have purpose, our worries and anxieties are given a proper perspective. God is the one on the throne; we are not.

Think about it. We worry about things that are out of our control because they are out of our control. We worry about our limitations and our shortcomings. We worry about troubles that are far beyond our ability to fix them. And when we claim to be Christ followers, worrying about the things of this world is a failure in the test of trust. Do we trust that God truly works out all things for good for those who love Him (Romans 8:28)? Are we willing to concede control over our lives and trust the One who has the power to control and hold together the entire universe of which we are a part?

A life lived out of this foundation is a life that is others-focused, others-minded, and truly an embodiment of Christ-like love. When the matters of our heart are aligned with the heart of God, our lives will be better than we could have ever imagined, no matter our situations, no matter our limitations. We'll live for Him, not for fame or fortune, not for compliments or comfort, but for Him and Him alone.

CHAPTER 8

# THROUGH THE EYE OF A HURRICANE

---

*Those who aren't following Jesus aren't his followers. It's that simple. Followers follow, and those who don't follow aren't followers. To follow Jesus means to follow Jesus into a society where justice rules, where love shapes everything. To follow Jesus means to take up his dream and work for it. — Scot McKnight*

"Gold! Gold! Gold from the American River!"[6] shouted Samuel Brannan. It was March of 1848 when Brannan shouted those words. He was in the middle of the gold rush that sent thousands of people west in hopes of finding gold and making it big. People left everything they knew. Some found a better life. Others found nothing.

---

[6] Bancroft, Hubert Howe (1888), pp. 55–56.

So, what propelled thousands of people to leave everything they knew, to lose everything, and to move to the wild west? One word: hope. It wasn't the gold – they didn't have it yet and there were no guarantees they were going to find any. Hope is what sent thousands of people west. They heard that gold was there, and they had a spark of hope ignite within them that tomorrow could be better than yesterday. Hope is what kept them going west when travels got tough. Hope is what kept them looking when, day after day, they found nothing. Hope is what kept them sustained in the midst of adversity.

While we don't have a gold rush today that is sending people all over the country in search of a better life, we do have the opportunity to declare a "new gold rush," one that will bring about more hope in the hearts and souls of people than ever before.

## A NEW GOLD RUSH

It's one of the simplest statements, yet one of the hardest to live out. You've probably heard it many times, either from Scripture or from the mouths of your parents. It has many versions, but it originated with Jesus. It is the bottom line in Jesus' way of life. Here's what it is: "So whatever you wish that others would do to you, do also to them, for this is the Law and the Prophets" (Matthew 7:12). You may know this as the "golden rule," but I want you to refer to it now as the "new gold rush." Just imagine what it would be like if that statement became reality in our lives.

With the relentless love of God being thrown down on us, it should be quite easy for us to know how living out this verse would impact others. In a world that is a constant place of dysfunction, discord, and disunity, God's people *must* begin to exhibit a new gold rush in their hearts, minds, and lives. And make no mistake, "God's people" begins with you and me. We need not wait for anyone else to tell us to love others. God's word is clear to us here and now.

How would you like to be treated? Like you don't matter? Like you have no value? Like you're a burden? Like you're an annoyance? Obviously not. And yet, this is how we often treat others in our lives. Instead, wouldn't you rather be treated with kindness, respect, and most of all, love? We all want to be valued and thought of positively. These aren't bad desires. Instead, they give us a clear picture as to how we should treat others. If a person has any semblance of self-respect, it's easy to see how this principle applies to our lives.

In every moment, imagine how you could live this out. How would you want to be treated by *them?* Then go and do likewise. The impact of this will be far and wide because it will begin a ripple effect of more and more people doing it as well. The gold rush of the 1800's gave hope to thousands, but this new gold rush has the potential to give hope to billions. In fact, the new gold rush movement is in full motion. The movement is strong and it has been going on for centuries now. People all over this world, every day, are responding to the gospel of Christ because someone decided to shower them with this golden love and to tell them where it comes from. Will you join in on this movement today too?

## Bumpy Roads Ahead

Look around. How many people in your life live with the kind of joy that propels them to treat others the way they desire to be treated? Likely what you see are many people who, at some point in the day, express the kinds of feelings toward others that would give them a near aneurism if they knew someone else felt the same way about them. You probably see many people willing to hold a grudge against you at the drop of a hat. Looking around, either right where you are or throughout your day, probably sheds some light on the path that most people take. Most aren't headed to the place of this new gold rush. Instead, they're headed down a path that is well traveled. This path they're on is easier, sure; but the path isn't better, by any means.

Jesus was clear about this. He went so far as to say that the wide, easy path is going to one destination: destruction. Here's what He said:

> [13] Enter by the narrow gate. For the gate is wide and the way is easy that leads to destruction, and those who enter by it are many. [14] For the gate is narrow and the way is hard that leads to life, and those who find it are few. — Matthew 7:13-14

The imagery would have been powerful for His disciples because they knew gates quite well. Cities were usually fortified with walls and gates. And Jesus equates His way, the way of the crucified, with a narrow gate and a hard path. The wide gate and easy path is the one most people take. But not you, He says. The way of the crucified is difficult because it is constantly requiring us to deny ourselves. The narrow gate is designated for those who have decided in their minds and in their hearts that God's desires for them are paramount. Even more, the narrow gate is designated for those who have surrendered to Jesus and have been indwelled by the Spirit of God. For without the Spirit of God guiding us, molding us, and teaching us, we would be left to ourselves and would eventually shift toward the easy path.

The way of the crucified follows a hard path that has a narrow gate. It's hard because it doesn't serve self; it's designed to serve others no matter the cost to self. It's narrow because many opt for a life of comfort, following the easy path that is taken by the masses.

This new gold rush – a movement of Christ-centered love working through us and toward others – requires us to put our focus on our Savior and not on our surroundings. This is the only way to walk the hard path of the crucified. Our eyes are up, our focus is on the One who is showing us, every day, how to treat others the way we would like to be treated. He is going to the hurting and the desperate. He is bringing light to darkness. He is giving hope to all who are receptive to the good news. This is our Lord. This is our Savior. This is the path He is taking us on. He will lead us and will show us the way. We must simply open our eyes to see His priorities, and lay aside our own.

## How Are Your Roots?

It's not a profound insight that what lies beneath the surface eventually manifests to the surface. We've seen people who, on the outside, seemed to have it all together, only to later reveal that what was on the inside wasn't all that "together" after all. Just in the past couple of years, many well-known pastors of large churches have resigned or been let go because what was under the surface was harmful to their lives, families, and ministries. But the risk isn't just for pastors; we all can fall into this as well.

As we go about life with Christ, it's easy to fall into the trap of focusing on what we're doing at the expense of focusing on who we're getting to know. Jesus gives us the imagery of a path because we are all on a journey with Him. He is leading the way, not only ahead of us, but beside us as well. He can show us the way and help us along the way, simultaneously. Jesus is present like that. His desire is not for us to simply do godly things, but for us to go on a journey *with* Him.

So, the question remains: *how are your roots?* How are you *really* doing deep down? How you answer that question is based on whether you are getting to know Christ or not. Maybe you're going through difficulties and you feel down and out. Maybe because of those difficulties, you'd say that you're not doing well deep down. I wouldn't blame you for thinking and believing that, but I would disagree with that being your reality.

We can go through our entire lives being tossed this way and that because of the winds and storms of our situations. It's certainly possible to do it. But what is really happening is a failure to know Christ and His life of abundance for you. The result of knowing Christ deeply is a rooted foundation in Him, not in our circumstances.

Whenever I am struggling with worry because of difficulties I am facing on this earth, I must take a step back and evaluate where my hope is really going. If I allow the difficulties of this world to sway me back and forth, I'm not giving my hope and trust to Christ; I'm giving it to this world. You and I both have the ability and opportunity to place our hope and trust in any direction we choose. Whenever we place them in the things of this world – our reputation, our prestige, our accomplishments, our family, our friends, our career, our bank account, etc. – we are setting ourselves up for a rapid fall because we are enabling our roots to rot away.

A quick test to determine if our roots are being nourished by knowing Christ is to simply ask this question: *what is currently causing me to rejoice?* To rejoice is to express the joy we have. We all experience joy at one point or another, but where that joy comes from says a lot about what we truly value in life. If the only thing causing you to rejoice is the raise you got at work, your career may be the highest priority. Yikes. If many things cause you to rejoice and yet not one of them is Christ, then there's a problem. As soon as our circumstances change, our joy can easily turn into misery. A sure sign that your roots are being nourished by knowing Christ is to determine whether or not God's word and His will cause you to rejoice.

## Know and Known

Jesus makes two statements that are intimately related to this as He sets up His conversation about our roots. First, He tells His disciples (and us) to watch out for false prophets. These are people who will come into your life and the life of your local church and will begin teaching what they believe. They'll likely be good teachers, but the content of what they teach will be slightly off. But more than that, the way to determine if someone is a false prophet is to examine their fruit. "You will recognize them by their fruits. Are grapes gathered from thornbushes, or figs from thistles?" (Matthew 7:16). This is Jesus' way of saying that whatever is below the surface will eventually make itself known.

Jesus' point isn't necessarily that false prophets are automatically theologically wrong, but that they are inwardly corrupt. A false prophet can be someone who has accurate theology, and yet doesn't truly know Christ. But don't automatically assume that this is simply a conversation about *other people*.

Jesus' second statement is quite scary. Just look at this: "Not everyone who says to me, 'Lord, Lord,' will enter the kingdom of heaven, but the one who does the will of my Father who is in heaven" (Matthew 7:21). He goes on to depict a hypothetical conversation where those who are not admitted to the kingdom of heaven claim to have done all these great things in Jesus' name. But Jesus' response to them is, "I never knew you; depart from me, you workers of lawlessness" (Matthew 7:23). Wow.

The sense I get from these two statements is that we can do the things that Christ desires for us to do without actually knowing Christ Himself. This is why, in our efforts of living for God, we can never forget to spend time getting to know God. Knowing God is at the foundation of everything we do. It is from the overflow of our relationship with Him that we do things for Him. If we spend the time investing in our relationship with God, our joy will be found in Him. Our hopes, dreams, and desires will begin to be transformed into His hopes, His dreams, and His desires. And out of that, we will live our lives for Him, walking in the narrow way of the crucified.

## A HURRICANE IS COMING

The old saying goes, you're either in a storm, coming out of a storm, or about to go into a storm. Unfortunately, we know this to be true, don't we? But in a world that is passing away, we shouldn't expect anything different. Not only is it difficult to live in this world because of the natural things that come about, but we also have an enemy who is trying to knock us down every chance he gets.

So, here's your warning: a hurricane is coming. The ball is in your court. How will you ensure that the hurricane doesn't rock your world to the point that you are thrust off your foundation and into destruction? Luckily you're not left to yourself to answer this question. Jesus gives us the recipe for getting through the hurricane successfully.

With His disciples leaning in, not knowing what else He would say, Jesus says, "Everyone then who hears these words of mine and does them will be like a wise man who built his house on the rock" (Matthew 7:24). It doesn't matter how nice this man's house is if he builds it on a sub-par foundation. The same is true about our lives. It doesn't matter if we accomplish a lot, accumulate a lot, or reach the pinnacle of happiness; if we haven't built our lives on a firm foundation, we'll be washed away when the hurricane comes.

With that statement, Jesus goes into a story about two types of people. The first are those who have heard His words and have done what He has said to do. They have not only responded in faith to His call to repentance, but they have come to faith in Him as well. They have experienced the joy of being crucified to life and now walk in their identity along the way of the crucified. They have laid their desires and dreams at the foot of the cross and have taken hold of Christ's desires and dreams. They have ultimately built their lives on a foundation of rock, found only in Christ. The second type of people are those who have heard Jesus' words but have *not* done what He has said to do. They have not responded in faith to His call to repentance. They have chosen to seek their own desires and dreams in place of Christ's. The problem was that this choice in life didn't serve them well in any way. When the hurricane came, they were washed away because their lives were on a foundation of sand, which shifts and settles in response to its surroundings.

## Roots Without Water

Jesus' point is clear: surviving the storms of life is dependent upon listening to His words and following them accordingly. The biggest problem we face as Christians in the modern world is two-fold: many of us don't know God's Word enough to even know what Jesus' words are, and for those who do know His words, too many don't follow them. In the eye of the storms of life, we often resort to our own opinions of things. Instead of loving our enemies and praying for them, we turn to hate and a desire for their destruction. Instead of living as heirs to the kingdom and adopting a life of meekness, we resort to wielding whatever power we have to keep ourselves safe and secure.

Whenever we resort to our own ideas and our own strength, we undercut the important work that Christ is doing in our lives through the eye of the hurricanes of life. Make no mistake, the difficulties you face serve a greater purpose than what is on the surface. It's through those difficulties that we can see whether or not we trust God. It's through the storms of life that we discover what our foundation is really like.

If you've ever planted a tree, you know that it needs to be supported to stand until its roots begin to develop below ground. If a storm comes before your new tree is firmly rooted in the ground, your tree will likely get harmed. After that tree is firmly rooted, however, it can withstand the storms it will face. But for its roots to expand and grab, it needs a steady diet of water. If it gets what it needs, it will flourish quickly. If it doesn't, it will die. We're surprisingly similar to a tree planted in the ground.

We all have some sort of a root system. In other words, we all have beliefs that keep us grounded in this world. Some of us have a root system that is faulty and incomplete, whereas others have taken Jesus' words to heart and have developed a root system that is not only intricate and dependable, but is nestled in soil that is dependable and firm as well. And just like a tree needs water for it to grow and develop to eventually grow above the surface, we need a steady diet of hearing Jesus' words and acting on them to experience our own growth as well.

## Rooted to Stand

Jesus' desire for us is to be so firmly planted in Him by always exercising our muscles of trust in Him that no matter what life throws at us, we can look to Him as our hope. The way of the crucified begins and ends in our reality as people who have been rescued, ransomed, and indwelled by the One True King, Jesus Christ. When we can allow the beauty of what Christ has done for and in us, we can begin to live lives where He is constantly working through us.

We have no better choice than to stand firm in God because every other option is fleeting, leading us to a demise of eternal proportions. So, as your next storm comes knocking on your door, don't lose confidence in the goodness of God. He is greater than any problem you face. He is infinitely more powerful than you worst weakness. If you let Him, He'll get you through the eye of the storm. And on the other side, you'll find that your character is more like His and your trust in Him is deeper and wider than ever before.

One of the greatest temptations you'll fight against in the storms of life is putting all your focus on the storms themselves. You'll be tempted to focus on yourself and only yourself. However, we must fight against the temptation because God does not see us through our storm so that we'll simply survive it, but so that we'll thrive in Him and in His mission in the midst of the storm.

We are rooted to stand so we can shine Christ's light to a dark and dying world. In every moment, in every situation, our priority must be on honoring God. And at the foundation of honoring God is loving Him and others. It could be that the person causing us to go through the storm we're in is the exact person God is calling us to love and lead to Him.

Can you imagine if we, God's Church, were to draw a line in the sand and become determined to love anyone and everyone no matter the problems we face? In my experience counseling people who struggle with the storms of life, I've encouraged them to find ways to get their focus off themselves. It's easy to fall into a rut where the hardships we face become preeminent in our minds, and the best way I know to fight against that is to love and serve someone else. This is something that I've had to implement in my own life on many occasions. When I feel down or sorry for myself – regardless of the reasons – and I shift my focus toward someone else and seek to encourage him or her in some way, I can't tell you how fast my sadness and discouragement transform into a deep sense of purpose. But why is that? When we not only hear Jesus' words, but also act on them, we experience a deep sense of purpose, because it is in those moments that we are living in His will for our lives.

## STAY ASTONISHED

Jesus' sermon on the mountainside was not only to His disciples sitting at His feet, but it was to the crowds who were standing and sitting in the distance as well. As He concluded His message to them, people began to realize that this Rabbi was different from all the others. People began to realize that He had an authority that was like no other. And as they continued to follow Jesus from town to town, witnessing healings, teachings, and miracles, people began to realize that this Jesus was God in flesh.

This is what happens when we have an encounter with the real Jesus who came to give us abundant life: He leaves us astonished and wanting more. And it's that posture, that attitude, that we should keep. Consider the crowds' response:

> [28] And when Jesus finished these sayings, the crowds were astonished at his teaching, [29] for he was teaching them as one who had authority, and not as their scribes. – Matthew 7:28-29

The crowds were astonished at Jesus' teaching and we should be as well, because as soon as we begin to follow His way, we realize that we need Him even more. But we aren't only astonished at Jesus' teaching, for we know that He was much more than just a teacher; He was, and is, the crucified God. He is the Almighty who took on flesh, like you and me, and gave Himself up to death so that we could have life. He is the resurrected King who defeated death and sin. He is our Rescuer who set us free from our old ways by putting our old selves to death and raising us anew in Himself. He is the Creator of the universe who looked upon us and declared, *that'll do*. He is the God who is all-present and who has put His Spirit in us, making us the very temple of God. He is our loving King who has given us a mission in life that is filled with purpose. He is our Redeemer who will return to wipe away every tear and to make everything brand new.

Jesus' desire for us all, as we embark on this journey of living as the crucified, is for us to stay astonished at His power, His grace, His holiness, His love, and everything else about Him. When we stay astonished at who He is, we remain in the proper posture toward Him and refuse to put our hope in ourselves. Staying astonished at who He is allows us to keep our perspective in check when life's difficulties begin to mount. It propels us to prayer. It guides us to humility. It reminds us of what Christ has done and is doing in our lives.

No matter what we face, no matter what or who opposes us, we can remain hope-filled people. We can remain people of peace because the God of peace is with us and in us. We can walk as those who will radically love our enemies because we know that what is here and now is not the end of the story. We know that the present struggles are not to be compared with the glory that awaits us. We are the crucified. We are the Church. We are God's children who are heirs to the kingdom of heaven. And because of that, we walk in the way of the crucified. Every moment of every day we walk, we serve, we love, we hope, and we honor our God and King who is on the throne.

Dear reader,

Thank you for investing in your walk with God. My hope is that the Scriptures we looked at together have been used by the Spirit of God to speak directly to you. As you continue in your journey, I'd love to hear how God is working in your life. You can contact me directly at BrandonKelley.org. May God bless you every day you walk with Him.

In Christ,
Brandon Kelley
#CrucifiedtoLife

## Free Bonus Resources

For all readers: If you would like to dive deeper into this journey of the abundant life, grab your copy of the *Crucified to Life 30-Day Bible Reading Plan*. You can get it by going to BrandonKelley.org/bonus.

For pastors: If you would like to share *Crucified to Life* with your congregation, you'll want to get your copy of the *Crucified to Life Sermon Series Pack*. In it are four message outlines and all the graphics you need to help your congregation live abundant life in Christ. You can get it by going to BrandonKelley.org/pastors.

Made in the USA
San Bernardino, CA
14 March 2017